BACKYARD BIRD IDENTIFICATION GUIDE

Jerry G. Walls

Photo Credits:

Ron Austing: *p. 1 (Tufted Titmouse); 15 (Gambel's Quail); 16 (American Goldfinch); 18; 25T; 29; 34 all; 36T & B; 37T & C; 38T; 40C; 41C & B; 43T & B; 45T; 46B; 47B; 48T & C; 49T & C; 50T & C; 51 all; 52C & B; 53 all; 54B; 55B; 56B; 57C & B; 58T & C; 59C; 61T & C; 62C; 63T*

Jeff Fishbein: *p. 47C; 59T; 60T*

Marvin Hyett: *p. 3 (Vermilion Flycatcher); 11T; 19*

Larry Kimball: *p. 24B; 25B; 27; 28 all; 32; 37B; 38B; 39B; 42C; 44C; 56C; 60C; 62T; 63C*

Larry Kimball & Barbara Magnuson: *p. 49B*

Peter LaTourette: *p. 5 (Yellow-rumped Warbler); 12; 35B; 36C; 40T & B; 41T; 42T; 44B; 45C; 46C; 48B; 50 B; 52T; 57T; 58B*

Barbara Magnuson: *p. 6T; 17 (Broad-tailed Hummingbird); 23 (Yellow-headed Blackbird); 26; 39C; 45B;55C; 62B*

Rafi Reyes: *p. 5; 10 all*

Rob & Ann Simpson: *p. 6B; 7; 8; 9 (Cedar Waxwing); 14; 20; 21; 22; 30; 33; 35T & C; 38C; 39T; 42B; 43C; 44T; 47 T; 54T & C; 55T; 56T; 59B; 60B; 61B; 63B*

John Tyson: *p. 24T; 31 (Tufted Titmouse); 46T*

Dedication

For Maleta, with love

KT 103

Distributed in the UNITED STATES to the Pet Trade by T.F.H. Publications, Inc., 1 TFH Plaza, Neptune City, NJ 07753; on the Internet at www.tfh.com; in CANADA by Rolf C. Hagen Inc., 3225 Sartelon St., Montreal, Quebec H4R 1E8; Pet Trade by H & L Pet Supplies Inc., 27 Kingston Crescent, Kitchener, Ontario N2B 2T6; in ENGLAND by T.F.H. Publications, PO Box 74, Havant PO9 5TT; in AUSTRALIA AND THE SOUTH PACIFIC by T.F.H. (Australia), Pty. Ltd., Box 149, Brookvale 2100 N.S.W., Australia; in NEW ZEALAND by Brooklands Aquarium Ltd., 5 McGiven Drive, New Plymouth, RD1 New Zealand; in SOUTH AFRICA by Rolf C. Hagen S.A. (PTY.) LTD., P.O. Box 201199, Durban North 4016, South Africa; in JAPAN by T.F.H. Publications. Published by T.F.H. Publications, Inc.

Manufactured in the

United States of America

by T.F.H. Publications, Inc.

CONTENTS

BIRDWATCHING: A GROWING HOBBY 5

1 BINOCULARS, BOOKS, AND TAPES 9

2 WHAT TO LOOK FOR 15

3 COMMON BIRD FAMILIES 23

4 IDENTIFYING COMMON BIRDS 31

INDEX 64

Birdwatching is a hobby that can appeal to all ages and all income groups in any part of the country.

Introduction

BIRDWATCHING: A GROWING HOBBY

If you have picked up a copy of this book, you probably want to put a correct name on the birds that are coming to your feeders each day. You've become a birdwatcher rather than just a birdfeeder—you not only want to have birds coming to your yard, but you want to know what they are called.

There are well over 800 distinct kinds (species) of birds known from North America, basically the United States and Canada. Of these, at least 600 are relatively findable if you travel about the U.S., and over a decade or more and a lot of birdwatching trips, you could see over 700 species. Almost every state has at least 300 to 400 species of birds recorded from

The Bridled Titmouse of the southwestern U.S. and Mexico formerly was called Parus wollweberi, *but today it carries the scientific name* Baeolophus wollweberi.

within its borders, and it is not uncommon for a single yard situated near a productive body of water to attract more than a hundred species over a period of a few years. Birds are everywhere, they often are extremely abundant, and many are loud and colorful.

The Importance of Names

Once you take the step of asking the correct name for that little gray or brown or yellow bird hanging from your feeder, you become empowered to answer all your other questions about the bird. Without knowing the name of a bird, you won't be able to find out more about how that bird breeds, what it feeds its young, or where it spends the winter or summer.

You will notice that birds, like other animals and plants, usually have two types of names. The one most birdwatchers use is the common name, an English name that has developed and become familiar through use for sometimes hundreds of years. The other type of name attached to all birds is the scientific name, which is formed by following a complicated set of rules. Though we will give the scientific name with each major species later in this book, the common name does very well for almost all bird talk and is the one used by your average birder.

Red-breasted Nuthatches breed in northern forests and high mountains, but in the winter they may appear almost anywhere.

Lists

Once you know the correct name for that little visitor, you probably will want to jot it down somewhere so you have it next time the bird appears. This is the natural beginning of listing, and it can quickly grow in scope. First you will develop a "yard list," a simple listing of the birds that come to your feeders, sing from the trees during migration, or even fly by overhead. Yard lists often begin with the dozen most common year-round (resident) species such as House Sparrow, House Finch, and Northern Cardinal, growing rapidly with the addition of more species during the winter. Even in a distinctly urban area it is not uncommon for 40 or 50 species to appear in a yard over the course of a year, and over a decade or more you could easily get 100 species.

Your enthusiasm and growing experience may lead you to venture further afield after new species to observe, and you will want to keep track of what you see. This leads to the development of other lists, usually including a "life list" in which all the species you identify at home and in your travels are recorded. Today there are several journal-type books available that allow you to record your sightings species by species, often with details of when and where you first saw the bird.

TO LIST OR NOT TO LIST

Some people disdain listing—they say that the list becomes more important than the birds seen. This does happen, but it need not. Keeping a list can be important for many reasons, the prime one of which is to jog and check your memory. After you have seen 200 or so birds, details often begin to become jumbled. Just when did you see your first Scarlet Tanager and where? By keeping a list, all the basic information on what you've seen and where and when you first saw it is readily available.

Without a list you may not remember if you have seen only the Chipping Sparrow (top) or also the Clay-colored Sparrow (bottom), two very similar birds.

A stunning male Scarlet Tanager.

Chapter One

BINOCULARS, BOOKS, AND TAPES

As with any hobby, to fully enjoy it you must have the proper equipment. In the case of watching birds, this must at a minimum consist of a good pair of binoculars and at least one field guide to aid more complicated identifications. As you progress, you will probably also want tapes of bird songs. Kept to a minimum, you can do a lot of enjoyable watching for just a small investment.

Bins

Birders have adopted the abbreviation "bins" for binoculars, the paired tubes that are essential for really seeing a bird clearly. Binoculars are available in dozens of models and price ranges, from inexpensive

Porro prism style binoculars still are the most commonly used bins and often the cheapest for their quality.

toys to precision instruments that cost a month's wages and will survive being dropped off a cliff. What you want is something between these extremes.

Two styles of binoculars compete in the market. In the traditional type, the porro prism style, there are pairs of prisms set at an angle to the lenses that you put to your eyes (the oculars or eyepieces). Porro prism bins are relatively wide and distinctly shouldered over the prisms. Roof prisms are more complicated internally in their prisms but externally appear as two simple tubes with lenses at each end. Most bins you see for sale in department stores will be porro prisms, while most of the very expensive models sold in birding specialty shops and catalogs will be roof prisms.

All bins are rated by a pair of numbers, the 7x35, 9x50, 8x21, etc., that you see on the labels. The first number is the magnification of the binoculars—how many times larger the bird will appear through the bins than through the naked eye. For casual birding, most enthusiasts probably prefer a moderate magnification of 7 or 8 as this gives you a wide field of view (distance seen from edge to edge when you look through the binoculars) to more easily follow and find small, moving birds. Higher powers may give more detail but also tend to be heavier and often more expensive as well as giving you a more restricted field of view. If you will be looking at birds mostly in trees, shrubs, and fields, 7-power bins will do you well. If you expect to be looking at shorebirds, ducks, and other birds at distances over water, you might find a 9- or 10-power binocular better in the long run. Magnifications below 7 and above 10 are not practical for most birdwatching.

Spotting scopes are expensive but useful if you bird near water or want to study the finest details of birds.

The second number is aperture, reflecting the size of the objective lens (the lenses at the far end of the tubes). The smaller this lens, the less light enters the binoculars and the darker the image will appear. With porro prisms, apertures under 35 will not allow you to determine colors and in dim light you might well see nothing at all. An aperture of 50 or up often is called a "night lens," but this offers little advantage to average birdwatching. Roof prisms tend to have smaller aperture numbers than porro prisms and must be judged differently. An aperture of 21 to 30 is good for most birding when using a roof prism. A porro prism of 7x35 to 8x50 is fine for birdwatching; the roof equivalents would be between 7x21 and 8x35.

Nervous birds of dark forests, such as the Red-eyed Vireo, are best seen with bins of lower power and wide aperture.

Look for binoculars with a central focusing knob and one movable eyepiece that can be set to allow for differences between your left and right eyes. Most bins also have rubber cups around the eyepieces that can be folded down to allow a clearer, wider view if you look through eyeglasses.

Weight is an important consideration when buying bins, as is simply the feel of the instrument in your hands. Most full-size binoculars weigh

A gourmet mix of ingredients will help you attract a wide variety of garden birds such as cardinals, finches, and sparrows. Photo courtesy of Kaytee® Products, Inc.

about a pound and a half or so, which doesn't seem like much until you carry one on a strap around your neck for hours at a time. By the way, spend a few dollars on a wide flexible foam strap; this accessory may be the most important you will ever buy.

Compact binoculars are smaller and lighter than full-size binoculars but tend to have smaller objective lenses and thus offer a darker image. They also seldom are as sturdily built as regular bins. An excellent compact binocular by a good manufacturer will cost as much or more than an equivalent full-size binocular in many cases, and cheap compacts usually are just toys. If you buy compacts, stick to a well-known brand and judge its optical qualities carefully, especially the brightness of the view.

The Printed Word — and Pictures

This book gives you enough information to correctly identify several dozen bird species, but even casual birdwatching will bring you into contact with dozens or even hundreds more species. To identify these you need an inexpensive but essential book known as a field guide. Spend the money early in your hobby and enjoy it more.

Currently there are at least three major bird field guides available that cover the bird species of either the entirety of the U.S. and Canada or the eastern and western regions of the same area. Because birds fly and often

Even common birds such as the Song Sparrow may require that you note subtle characters to be sure of your identification. Field guides are excellent fast references for such characters and good memory joggers.

appear in unexpected areas thousands of miles from where they should be, a guide that covers the entire country is more authoritative than one that may lack a species that appears at your feeder one winter when it should really be on the opposite coast. However, regional guides give the beginner fewer species to become used to as their interest and skill develop, which may be an advantage.

Learning to Listen

"Birding by ear" is achieved by those birders who have developed a memory of the different songs and call notes of dozens or perhaps hundreds of birds and also the ability to pick these notes from the background hubbub and arrive at a correct identification.

All birds produce a variety of sounds depending on sex, age, season, and activity, but most songbirds have characteristic calls that they give to identify themselves to others of their own species. Through the miracles of modern technology, almost all these sounds are easily available on tape or CD for you to listen to and study at your leisure. Some of these recordings are accompanied by manuals that tell you what to listen for to distinguish similar-sounding species.

DO YOU NEED A SCOPE?

If you go on any birdwatching trips, you are sure to see several people using spotting telescopes on tripods to observe distant birds. These little telescopes usually magnify an image between 15 and 60 times, depending on the lenses being used, and are almost necessary if you chase rare birds or do much watching near large bodies of water. Unfortunately, they are heavy and hard to use without a stable tripod. For most birdwatching, a good pair of bins is sufficient.

There are many choices of birdseed, from basic mixes to specialty blends, from bags to buckets or bells to cakes. Photo courtesy of Kaytee® Products, Inc.

The bright yellow lores of this adult White-throated Sparrow are a good character to help your identification.

Chapter Two

WHAT TO LOOK FOR

Many people who have never tried to accurately identify birds think that, because birds are common, fairly large, and often colorful, they are easy to identify. Unfortunately, birds are confusingly similar, very variable with sex, season, and sometimes range, and often are hard to observe in detail. Add to these factors the simple fact that to identify a bird you have to know just what features are important to tell them apart, and you can have a very complicated situation.

Much of bird identification is comparative, so you can get a good start by learning in detail the birds you see every day at your feeders or in the yard. You then

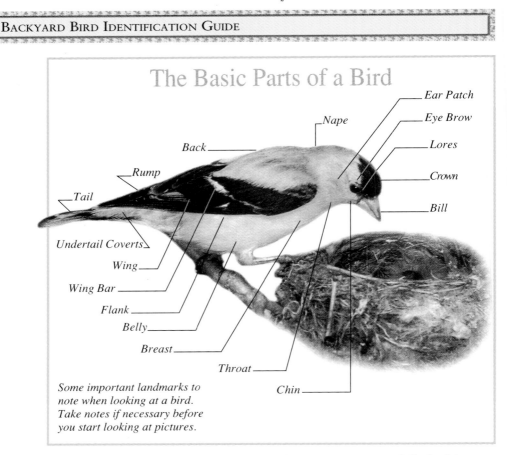

The Basic Parts of a Bird

Ear Patch
Nape
Eye Brow
Back
Lores
Rump
Crown
Tail
Bill
Undertail Coverts
Wing
Wing Bar
Flank
Belly
Breast
Throat
Chin

Some important landmarks to note when looking at a bird. Take notes if necessary before you start looking at pictures.

build on this base by adding more and more species, carefully looking at each species and making mental (and sometimes written) notes on just what makes them the species they are. If you learn how to recognize a House Finch, for instance, it doesn't take much experience to see that a Purple Finch at your feeder is different in details of color, pattern, and even shape. You should be able to tell they are related birds, however, by noticing the similar bill shape, placement of the legs and wings, and just the general "feel."

Identification Clues

To identify a bird you have to look at structure, and to do this you need to know some basic terms for what you are looking at.

The majority of the birds in this book are songbirds, and they are built along very similar patterns. The major obvious differences are in the bill, which may vary from flat and wide as in the flycatchers through deep and heavy as in crows, to slender and sharply pointed in the blackbirds and relatives. Looking closely at the bill is always a good way to start an identification.

Descriptions of birds tend to follow a regular pattern and use similar names for the parts important to identification. The head, for instance, has many features. Its top is the crown, the sides the face, its back the

In hummingbirds, here a male Broad-tailed Hummingbird, the brilliant feathers on the throat are termed the gorget.

nape. The lores are the small area between the front of the eye and the base of the bill.

The area just under the base of the bill is the chin, followed by the throat. The breast (chest) is the area below the throat. Below this is the belly. The undertail coverts are the distinctive feathers from the vent back under the base of the tail. The sides of a bird are its flanks, usually considered to be the areas more or less below the edges of the folded wings. Together these areas are referred to here as the underparts.

The back extends from the nape (back of the neck) to the feathering just above the base of the tail, the rump. Commonly the rump is a contrasting color to the rest of the back, and the lower back may even be somewhat different in color from the more forward part of the back.

The tail may be short (usually half or less the length of the back) to long. It may end squarely, be rounded at the tip, or have a distinct shallow to deep notch caused by the center feathers being shorter than the outer feathers. Noting tail length and shape often is important in identification.

The wings are important structures in bird identification, but most of their characters concern details of feather length and shape visible only in-hand. Speaking in generalities, you will note three different regions on a bird's wing. The long outer feathers at the end of the wing are the primaries; the outermost primaries often extend beyond the other feathers, giving wings distinctive shapes. Interior to the primaries are the secondaries, which tend to be shorter and uniform in length, often not prominent in a sitting bird. Together the primaries and secondaries often are called the flight feathers. In a sitting bird with folded wings, the short feathers from the bend of the wing back to the bases of the primaries and secondaries form a series of covert feathers (primary, secondary, etc.). They often have colors and patterns that contrast with the flight feathers.

SEEING RED

Many people have asked where the red is on the belly of the Red-bellied Woodpecker, and some authors have answered that there is little or none and the common name is misleading. Actually, many Red-bellies have a large, very visible patch of rosy red on the lower belly extending onto the undertail coverts. If you look carefully at birds in the breeding season, it may be hard to miss the red belly.

Color is Key

If they were not different colors, many birds would be impossible to distinguish by sight alone because their structure is so similar within groups. Phoebes, for instance, would be virtually identical if painted black. Sometimes you will have to look for very small details to be certain of identifications.

When you look at a bird, first get a general impression of the color scheme. Are the underparts all one color from chin to undertail coverts, or are there obvious contrasts? Is there a dark band across the breast or a black patch (bib) over the throat onto the upper breast? Commonly there is a spot or stripe of bright colors on the crown or the crown itself may be a different color than the rest of the head. The eye may have a pale (or dark) stripe above it, the eye brow, or have a thin contrasting ring of color around it, the eye ring. There often is a darker patch just behind the eye, sometimes called an ear patch. Is the base of the bill or the lower mandible paler than the rest of the bill? Is there a

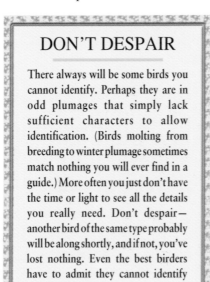

DON'T DESPAIR

There always will be some birds you cannot identify. Perhaps they are in odd plumages that simply lack sufficient characters to allow identification. (Birds molting from breeding to winter plumage sometimes match nothing you will ever find in a guide.) More often you just don't have the time or light to see all the details you really need. Don't despair— another bird of the same type probably will be along shortly, and if not, you've lost nothing. Even the best birders have to admit they cannot identify every bird they see.

Strongly contrasting black and white stripes near the eye are common in birds such this Red-breasted Nuthatch. Notice their exact position, width, and colors.

A male Bullock's Oriole has a mostly yellow head with narrow black areas. Contrast this with the closely related Baltimore Oriole.

darker area around the base of the bill? This may be called a mask, and it often extends back to the eye.

On the wings, look for pale horizontal or oblique bars, the wing bars. These generally occur as a pair, anterior (front) and posterior (back), but one may be absent or much larger and of a different color than the other. Wing bars often are white and sharp-edged, easy to see. Also notice if the edges of the primaries are paler than the rest of the feathering.

Try to watch the bird for a while as it moves a bit, presenting different parts of its body for close examination. If it tucks the head under the wing, notice if the underside of the wings (the lining) is brightly colored.

Behavior

Though they seldom are essential to identification, behavioral clues may make identification simpler or more certain. Of course, if you are looking at feeder birds you do not have the advantage of placing a bird in its natural habitat, and you seldom have a chance to see a bird's nest. However, you can look for twitches and movements to give you more material for making an identification.

Small birds often have characteristic twitches. Phoebes, for instance, jerk the tail up and down, called pumping. Wrens often hold the tail cocked over the back while scolding an intruder. Kinglets open and close the wings suddenly (twitching).

Flight often allows you to notice otherwise hidden colors. When Eastern Kingbirds soar out after insects, they spread the tail, displaying the broad white band across its end. The bright wing linings of Rose-breasted Grosbeaks and Northern Flickers are conspicuous and distinctive when the birds fly from tree to tree or feeder to feeder. Notice how the tail is held when the bird flies.

NESTING WRENS

Nine wren species nest in the United States, and they position their nests in four distinctive ways. House, Winter, Carolina, and Bewick's Wrens all construct their nests in cavities, originally holes in trees but today often in nest boxes and other man-made structures with narrow openings. Canyon and Rock Wrens also place their nests in cavities, but usually crevices in cliffs or between large rocks, even paving the entrance area with small stones. Marsh and Sedge Wrens build compact cups placed among rushes and sedges, males producing sometimes dozens of "dummy nests" that are never occupied. The Cactus Wren builds a nest a foot in diameter, protected by spiny plants such as cacti; the nest is used for years and serves as a roost.

Understanding What You See

To identify birds, you have to know what features to compare. You start this by studying the pictures in this book and the plates in the field guide that you may buy. Look at them often and closely, noting similarities between birds in the basic groups, families. All the warblers, for instance, share certain characteristics, and most have a similar appearance quite different from, say, sparrows. The blackbird family, regardless of color, generally has a similar look, often with a slender, sharply pointed bill much like that of the brightly colored orioles, which are indeed close relatives. Tanagers have heavy body builds and big bills with a small tooth on each side. Do your homework.

Make notes of what you see when you look at an unidentified bird. Carry a little notebook with you and a couple of pencils and jot down such things as wing bars, eye rings, bill shape, any contrasting colors on the rump or crown, tail pumping, wing twitching, etc. Make little sketches if these work better for you than words. You may have only a minute or less to look at a bird, so check as many features as possible and note them mentally until you can jot them down.

Try not to get into the bad habit of taking a glance at a bird and then starting to flip through a guide until you find a similar picture. First, you'll seldom find a good match right away. Second, the bird will be long gone by the time you look up again to check how it matches the picture. Look at the bird—it has all the characters you need to know about. You are identifying birds, not pictures.

Not all individual birds match field guide drawings or photos. This immature male Blue Grosbeak is molting its feathers and has the blue mostly confined to the head.

A male Baltimore Oriole has a completely black-hooded head. Until recently, the Baltimore and Bullock's Orioles were combined into a single species, the Northern Oriole. Increased knowledge often leads to different interpretations of species.

Ruby-crowned Kinglets may be mostly grayish green little birds, but males hide a fire-red crest on their heads.

Chapter Three

COMMON BIRD FAMILIES

Nortorth America has over 800 species of birds recorded from its borders (almost 900 if you count species from other areas that rarely cross over from Asia), from Alaska to the Mexican border. This represents less than 10 percent of the total number of birds known from all continents, currently over 9,000 species by some counts. Ornithologists (scientists who study birds) long have divided the birds into a number of closely related groups known as families. Though taxonomists (scientists who study identification and relationships of animals and plants) often argue about exactly which birds belong in a family and whether to recognize relatively fewer,

The Kestrel is a hawk-like bird that belongs to the family Falconidae, the falcons. Ornithologists today recognize over 70 bird families in North America.

larger families or more, smaller families, the general outlines of bird relationships are fairly clear today.

In North America there are some 74 families of native birds plus representatives of several families introduced from Europe. Many of the native families represent waterbirds, shorebirds, and groups that are unlikely to be found at feeders or near houses. Members of 25 native families plus two introduced families are discussed here, most of these perching birds, including the typical songbirds. In the following sections we'll briefly go through these families, trying to point out similarities among their members that may make it easier to place unidentified birds into small groups you can find more readily in the field guides. Bird families are defined scientifically by very technical characters, such as structure of the skeleton, ligaments in the legs, and coiling of the intestines, plus detailed structure of the feathers and how nestling develop. Few such characters can be appreciated through binoculars, so of necessity the following discussions are very superficial and non-technical.

Ducks to Woodpeckers

Of the birds covered in this book these are the most primitive. They stand in strong contrast to the remaining birds, the perching birds, which have more specialized foot and wing structure.

•Ducks and geese belong to the family Anatidae, an easily recognized worldwide group. These are large birds, few under a foot in length, and all with the bill flattened into the typical "duck beak." All have feet with three webbed toes to the front and a small free toe, the spur, at the back.

•Hawks and eagles, family Accipitridae, are another worldwide

The Mallard is a typical duck, family Anatidae, and one of the most widely distributed birds on Earth.

family of relatively large birds, few under a foot in length. The eyes look forward to give binocular vision, and the bill is relatively small but sharply hooked. The legs and feet are strong, the toes with very long, curved claws; the three front toes are set off from the hind toe, and two toes may be fused at their bases. Hawks are not related to owls, though they share a similar bill with a shared purpose; it is thought today that owls are related to cuckoos and roadrunners.

Female Bobwhites lack the contrasting head pattern of males, but their overall appearance still yells "quail."

•The American quails now are placed in their own family, Odontophoridae, closely related to the chickens, pheasants, and grouse (family Phasianidae). The quails are all chunky-bodied ground birds with a small tooth on each side of the bill.

•Pigeons and doves, family Columbidae, represent another large, worldwide family. Their small, soft bills are slightly narrower at the middle than the tip and there is a fleshy base around the nostrils. Pigeons and doves are not distinct scientific groups but common names for weakly distinguished assemblages. As a rule, pigeons are heavier-bodied than doves and have shorter, squared-off tails compared to the often longer, more pointed tails of doves.

•The amazing hummingbirds, family Trochilidae, are a strictly American group with dozens of species in the tropics, only a few ranging north into our borders. They generally are small to tiny birds with long, often strongly curved bills and tongues modified to feed on nectar deep within the bases of flowers.

•Woodpeckers, family Picidae, are uniquely adapted for feeding on insects under the bark and within the wood of trees. The feet have two strong-clawed toes pointing forward, two back (sometimes the fourth toe is lost), and the tail feathers have strong, spiny tips that help the bird sit vertically on a tree while pounding at the wood with the exceptionally tough bill.

The western Pygmy Nuthatch has a white face combined with a brown crown.

Flycatchers to Nuthatches

These families of perching birds usually are considered less modified than the families that follow because they lack certain developments of the wing feathers, but

MARTIN MYTH

In the southern United States many households have at least a few and often dozens of martin houses, and owners are proud to point out the Purple Martins that they draw. Though it is widely believed that Purple Martins eat tremendous numbers of mosquitoes, studies have shown that they feed on a variety of insects, with mosquitoes being much in the minority.

they all share feet modified to strong perching behavior. There are three toes pointing forward, one back, and there never is webbing between them. The structure of the ligaments in the legs clamps the toes closed around a branch until the bird consciously opens them, which is why perching birds often remain perched on their branch long after death.

•Tyrant flycatchers, family Tyrannidae, are an immense family of mostly greenish tropical American birds that feed on insects. The bill is flattened, quite wide at the base, with a small hook at the tip; there are hair-like feathers, rictal bristles, above the base of the bill.

•The jays and crows, as well as the magpies and ravens, belong to the family Corvidae. The crows are certainly among the largest perching birds, while the jays include some of the most colorful and personable. The bill in all is strong, with feathers extending beyond the nostrils.

•Swallows, family Hirundinidae, are perching birds that have developed long, pointed wings to aid in chasing and hawking for insects. The bill is broad at the base and there are rictal bristles that help direct insects into the mouth. The feet are small and weak, but swallows still spend much time perched on branches and power lines.

•Chickadees and titmice belong to the mostly Old World family Paridae. All are small, with short but strong bills and delicate-looking but strong feet. They often hang upside-down while feeding on seeds.

•The bushtits belong to the family Aegithalidae, a small group related to the chickadees but with longer tails and even smaller bills.

•Creepers, family Certhidae, are somewhat like streaky brown nuthatches that have become woodpeckers. The tail feathers end in spines that help the birds cling to tree trunks as in woodpeckers, but the bill is slender and curved to probe crevices in bark for small insects rather than digging into the wood.

•Nuthatches, family Sittidae, also are related to the chickadees, but like the creepers they are modified to pick insects from the trunks of trees. They have long or short, strong, pointed, straight bills and usually are blue-gray above with short tails.

This long-billed gray and black bird is a Clark's Nutcracker, a type of jay found in high mountains from western Canada to Mexico.

Wrens to Waxwings

The Cactus Wren is our largest wren and also the most contrastingly colored.

This grouping presents a variety of families of perching birds that are considered to be fairly highly modified, though they all have relatively simple feet and bills.

•The personable wrens form the family Troglodytidae, usually small to tiny birds with long, slightly curved bills and barred brownish coloration. The tail seems to be loosely attached to the body and often is held cocked over the back. They are loud, squeaky singers.

•Kinglets and gnatcatchers seem to be closely related to the Old World warblers, family Sylviidae, typical members of which occur in North America mostly as rarities in Alaska. Today kinglets are placed in their own family, Regulidae; there is little problem recognizing these tiny, fluffy, yet aggressive birds with bright colors on the crown. Gnatcatchers, which look like tiny mockingbirds, until recently were placed in their own family, Polioptilidae, where many specialists still feel they belong. Others feel they are highly modified American members of the family Sylviidae.

•The thrushes, family Turdidae, are the robins, bluebirds, and their relatives, a variety of fairly large perching birds with hundreds of species found almost everywhere. The family is very hard to define, and taxonomists are always quarreling about just what to include in it. The legs tend to be fairly long with strong feet; the birds often feed on the ground. The bill is moderately slender but strong and usually straight.

•The thrashers, family Mimidae, are a strictly American family closely related to the thrushes but often with a curved bill and brown to gray coloration. Mockingbirds and catbirds also belong in this family.

•Waxwings, family Bombycillidae, include just three species distributed around the Arctic Circle but often migrating far to the south. All are brown birds with short crests and short but strong bills. Red droplets of a waxy substance form at the tips of some of the wing feathers, a unique character of unknown function.

STATELY BIRDS

Northern Mockingbirds are a fixture of Deep South folklore and history and well-known and respected birds famous for their singing and mimicking abilities. This is the official state bird of Arkansas, Florida, Mississippi, Tennessee, and Texas. Curiously, the Brown Thrasher, which is reported to have over 1,100 recognizable songs, is the state bird only of Georgia. By the way, the Northern Cardinal is the state bird of seven states, the Western Meadowlark of six; American Goldfinch and American Robin score three states each, while two states (Delaware and Rhode Island) chose chickens as their state birds.

Few warblers come to feeders, so if you do not venture into the woods in spring you may never see a Yellow Warbler or any of its dozens of brilliant cousins.

Warblers to Blackbirds and Finches

Though a warbler bears little resemblance to a blackbird or a House Finch, scientists have believed these families to be so closely related that some have included them all in just one or two families. There are many groups that have characters intermediate between the major family groups, most of these restricted to tropical America.

• Wood-warblers, family Parulidae, seldom come to feeders, but they are prime birdwatching targets because of their often bright colors in the spring. They are small birds with typically slender, pointed black bills and fairly short tails.

• Tanagers, family Thraupidae, include hundreds of tropical American species, some among the most beautifully colored birds on the continent. Only a few reach North America, where they stand out by the bright colors of the breeding males and their thick bills with a distinct notch near the tip.

• Emberizidae includes the mostly American sparrows and their somewhat larger relatives the towhees, as well as the buntings of Europe

Sparrows are among the most difficult of birds to identify. The Field Sparrow is a common species with few identification marks other than the bright pastel bill.

and Asia. They tend to be birds with streaky, dull coloration and relatively thin though strong and conical bills.

•Cardinals and American buntings, including some of the birds called grosbeaks, form the family Cardinalidae. They often are larger than the related sparrows, with much deeper bills. Many are brightly colored.

•Though their slender, often slightly curved bills bear little resemblance to those of cardinals and sparrows, the blackbirds and orioles, family Icteridae, are thought to be closely related. A strictly American family, they vary from solid black birds through the streaky meadowlarks to the brilliant black and orange orioles.

•With the family Fringillidae, the true finches, we come to what are considered to be the most advanced American birds, a group that includes goldfinches, crossbills, grosbeaks, redpolls, and other finches that typically breed in the Far North, few extending into the tropics. All have thick, conical bills capable of cracking hard seeds, though in goldfinches, siskins, and redpolls the bill may be quite small.

DARLING STARLINGS

Though not greatly respected by American birders, the European Starling is a well-studied bird in Europe. It has complicated nesting behaviors, is an excellent mimic (it can learn to talk), and has unusual feeding behaviors. The bill muscles are modified to help the bill spring open with greater force than it shuts, letting the bird easily move plant leaves out of the way in its search for food. European Starlings are such well-adapted birds that the 60 introduced into Central Park only a century ago have grown into an estimated 200 million today.

Starlings and Old World Sparrows

These two families do not occur naturally in North America, but today their species may be the most abundant backyard birds on the continent.

House Sparrows may be abundant and are non-native, but they still are interesting birds that can be fun to watch.

•Starlings, family Sturnidae, are an Old World family somewhat related to the thrushes. They include a great diversity of body shapes and color patterns. Placed here are not only the familiar European Starling, a pesty tree hole nester, but the mynahs, noted for their loud voices and love of fruit.

•The abundant House Sparrow, a native of Europe and Asia, long was included in the weaver finch family, Ploceidae, but recently it has been placed in a distinctive family, Passeridae. These finches have conical bills and come in a variety of colors and patterns, though most species of the family look much like House Sparrows.

The rich tones of the Fox Sparrow help make it one of our most attractive birds.

Chapter Four

IDENTIFYING COMMON BIRDS

The following selection of North American birds represents mostly wide-ranging, common species likely to be found seasonally anywhere in the United States and southern Canada, plus species with smaller geographical ranges but of potential interest to a birdwatcher. An attempt has been made to represent all regions of the country, but fewer than 100 species out of a national list of 800 cannot be comprehensive.

The birds are presented more or less in AOU (American Ornithological Union) sequence, which is though to represent actual relationships of the birds. There are some deviations from AOU sequence to put similar-

FOLLOWING THE GUIDE

In each discussion, the same sequence is followed:
• A capsule description of the bird, emphasizing obvious characters of use in identification; females and young are briefly mentioned if they are obviously different from the breeding male.
• Voice is hard to describe, but where possible a written translation of what a song sounds like to at least some observers is given.
• Behavior mentions various topics of possible help in identification or appreciation of a bird.
• Attracting and feeding give a brief review of how likely a bird is to show up at a feeder, in what season, and what it probably will look for.
• Range generally includes brief outlines of both breeding and wintering ranges.
Because of space restrictions, none of these sections can be comprehensive, so you should always refer to a good field guide to be confident of your identification or to follow up on questions of behavior.

looking birds together. Thus Summer Tanager is discussed near Northern Cardinal rather than with other tanagers, while Vermilion Flycatcher is presented near Scarlet Tanager because beginners often confuse the males of these species.

You will note that not all these birds are really going to be found in a typical backyard. Birdwatching is a pastime that can quickly grow to an enjoyable addiction, and the author expects that you will soon want to leave your yard to search for new birds in local parks and pastures.

Space limitations prevent the discussion of many common birds, such as the Wood Duck, in this book. For more information, be sure to buy a good field guide.

Brown Thrashers are closely related to the Northern Mockingbird though very different in colors. Often the shape of a bird is as important as color in helping identify it.

Canada Goose • *Branta canadensis*

What to look for: A very large (30 to 40 inches long), long-necked goose. The head and neck are black with a wide white band (chinstrap) running from side to side under the throat to behind each eye.

Voice: A loud "honk" (especially in females); aggressive males may hiss.

Behavior: Typically noted flying overhead in large V formations or wandering lawns and marshes during the day. Once breeding mostly across Canada and the northern U.S., Canada Geese have established resident breeding groups over much of the U.S., especially in parks and near large lawns and golf courses. Males (larger than females, with thicker necks) may be very aggressive, especially when protecting a family group of females and young; keep your distance.

Attracting and feeding: Canada Geese feed on a variety of small mollusks, crustaceans, and other invertebrates taken in shallow water and also on grasses and their roots gleaned from lawns and the edge of water. Non-migratory populations are found on lawns and in parks all year and will take cracked corn and other grains.

Range: Wild birds breed across Canada and the northern U.S., migrating to the southern states for the winter.

Mallard • *Anas platyrhynchos*

What to look for: Occurring both as wild birds and almost identical cultivated forms. The male of this large (24 inches) duck has a metallic green head separated by a narrow white ring from a chestnut breast; the reflective bar at the edge of the wing (speculum) is bright blue with a narrow white bar on each side. Females are brown but have the same blue speculum as the male and white outer tail feathers.

Voice: One of the few ducks that really "quacks." Males are quieter than females and also have a low whistle.

Behavior: Commonly seen in large flocks in the winter, small numbers of wild birds often remain in parks and near water all year in much of the U.S.

Attracting and feeding: Mallards eat a tremendous variety of foods, from frogs and fishes through insects and snails to acorns, grasses, and grains. They are easy to attract to cracked corn and other common feeds on the ground.

Range: Found from coast to coast, but generally in the southern states only during the winter. Many northern individuals do not migrate if there is sufficient food during the winter.

Sharp-shinned Hawk • *Accipiter striatus*

What to look for: A true "chicken hawk," with a small head, long tail that is square across the tip, and long, slender orange legs that are naked below the thighs. Adults are 10 to 14 inches long and deep grayish blue above, white finely banded with red below, the crown the same color as the back; the eye is red. Juveniles are brown with a pale, heavily streaked head; the whitish underparts are spotted or streaked with reddish brown.

Voice: Generally silent, but can produce a quick series of "kek-kek" notes and a loud squeal.

Behavior: A breeding bird in dense forests, the short, wide wings giving it excellent mobility through branches. Hundreds of thousands migrate in large flocks along both coasts and along mountain ridges during autumn and spring. Individual birds often remain in the North through the winter.

Attracting and feeding: Sharp-shinned Hawks feed heavily on small birds, often near an active feeder, taking the occasional sparrow.

Range: A breeding bird over southern Canada and forests of northeastern and northwestern U.S., wintering from the central and southern U.S. into tropical America. The larger (14 to 20 inches) Cooper's Hawk has a rounded tail edged with white.

Northern Bobwhite • *Colinus virginianus*

What to look for: The only native quail in the eastern U.S. Usually about 9 inches long, it is a chunky, short-tailed ground bird with short wings. Males have a blackish head with a white stripe through the eye and a bright white throat; females have a brownish head and pale tan throat. In both sexes the back is streaked in shades of brown, while the belly is whitish with fine brown points and lines.

Voice: Males give a distinctive "bob-white" call that may be heard any time of the day. Some birds often produce only the first or last syllable, others add an "ah" before the call.

Behavior: Males, females, and juveniles unite in flocks or coveys of more than a dozen birds during the autumn and winter, pairs forming during March and April. Females virtually disappear while on the nest. The young are active enough to leave the nest an hour or two after hatching.

Attracting and feeding: Feeders placed near the edges of fields often attract Bobwhites. The birds come to cracked corn and other grains spread on or near the ground and may become regulars if fed at the same time each day.

Range: Found across the eastern U.S. from Texas to southern New England. The northern populations may die-out after several years of hard winters and today often trace their ancestry to birds introduced for hunting.

Scaled Quail • *Callipepla squamata*

What to look for: A 10-inch quail, often called the "Cottontop" because of the distinctive white-edged crest in both sexes and young. The breast and belly are bluish white with curved brown lines producing a fish-scale effect; the back is gray to brown. The head has only a weak dark stripe through the eye on a buffy background.

Voice: Not very vocal, but sometimes produces a low "pe-cos" and a soft "churr."

Behavior: A species of dry, often rocky prairies and scrublands, it may be seen along roads and field edges. Coveys of over a hundred birds may form in the autumn and winter, with breeding pairs getting together in the spring. As in other quail, the hatchlings can leave the nest as soon as their feathers dry.

Attracting and feeding: Scaled Quail prefer grass seeds to other foods but often will come to mixed seeds and finely ground corn given on the ground or on a low feeding table.

Range: Common from western Texas to southeastern Arizona, north into Colorado and Kansas and south into Mexico.

Gambel's Quail • *Callipepla gambelii*

What to look for: This large (10 to 11 inches) gray quail is one in which there is a long curved feather forming a topknot or plume. The plume turns forward and is wider and darker in males than females. Males have a black face and throat outlined with white, a white stripe through the eye, and a bright chestnut crown; there is a large black patch on the cream belly. Females are gray, with a paler throat and no contrasting head pattern. In both sexes there is a large chestnut patch on each flank below the wings.

Voice: A loud haunting, laughing "ha-haah-haaah" or a variable "khe-ca-go-go" with the accent on the second syllable.

Behavior: An abundant quail in dry habitats, including deserts, where there is a source of water, Gambel's Quail may form groups of dozens of birds all year, with even larger coveys in the cooler months. Males often call from trees and cacti 5 to 10 feet above the ground.

Attracting and feeding: Like many desert birds, Gambel's Quail will come to pans of water or a dripping hose placed near cover. They also take a variety of small seeds as well as softer foods. In nature they take soft leaves and buds as well as the usual seeds. Feeding birds often become very tame.

Range: The common quail of the deserts from extreme western Texas to southeastern California and southern Nevada. Along the Pacific Coast and Pacific Northwest it is replaced by the California Quail, which is browner on the back and crown and has a scaled pattern on the belly.

Rock Dove (Common Pigeon) • *Columba liva*

What to look for: Everyone recognizes the backyard pigeon, a foot-long, heavy-set bird introduced from Europe and now abundant in most cities. Coloration is extremely variable, but commonly the head and neck are darker gray than the body and there is a large iridescent patch on each side of the neck. Most Rock Doves show a white rump patch, not found in any native pigeon of similar size.

Voice: A soft "coo" often repeated in groups of four.

Behavior: Rock Doves form large feeding and roosting flocks and are excellent fliers, often seen gliding with the wings in a distinct V. Breeding takes place in old buildings, many birds nesting together. The wild Rock Dove frequented cliffs, and many of its behaviors still reflect the natural habitat.

Attracting and feeding: Flocks of pigeons often descend on feeders and feed of any type, wasting large amounts of seed and driving away smaller birds. In most areas the problem is keeping Rock Doves away from feeders, not attracting them.

Range: Found throughout the U.S. (native to southern Europe and Asia as well as Africa), they are almost always found near cities and farms, not in truly wild situations.

Mourning Dove • *Zenaida macroura*

What to look for: A slender, foot-long, pale grayish tan dove, pinkish buffy below. The head is small, and there usually is a curved dark spot well below the eye; males have a ring of blue skin around the eye that females usually lack and may have a pale violet spot on each side of the neck. The tail is long and pointed, with broad white edges to the feathers that are conspicuous in flight.

Voice: A loud, rolling "ooh-oo-woo-woo-woo" often confused by beginners with owl calls.

Behavior: Mourning Doves are likely to be found at feeders any time of the year. Quiet, gentle birds, they feed both on the ground and on feeding tables but seldom on hanging feeders. Their flight is fast and unpredictable, with a loud whirring when leaving the ground.

Attracting and feeding: Mourning Doves rapidly learn the location of feeders and will take a variety of small seeds. Their soft bills are not equipped for cracking sunflower hulls.

Range: One of the most common and widely distributed birds in North America, Mourning Doves are found from coast to coast and from southern Canada into tropical America. The related White-winged Dove of the southwestern states has a broad, curved white stripe across the center of the wing and a squarer tail.

Inca Dove • *Columbina inca*

What to look for: A small (8 inches), slender, delicate-looking ground dove, the Inca differs from related species in having a long, dark tail that is edged with white and has a rounded tip. The brown back feathers have dark edges producing a scaled effect; there is a large cinnamon patch in each wing.

Voice: Inca Doves produce a soft, simple "coo-coo" call.

Behavior: These are birds of open fields, parking lots, and parks, where they may form small feeding flocks.

Attracting and feeding: Like most other doves, Inca Doves take a variety of small seeds on the ground or a low feeding table.

Range: Inca Doves may be common across the Southwest, from eastern California to the Louisiana border and into Mexico. The range slowly is expanding to the north and east, and populations may be found in parks outside the main range.

Ruby-throated Hummingbird • *Archilochus colubris*

What to look for: The only hummingbird found east of the Mississippi River (except during the winter). Adults are less than 4 inches long, have a slender, almost straight bill, and are shiny green on the back. Females have a white throat, a buffy area on the flanks, and white tips to some of the tail feathers. Males have a broad bright red patch across the throat (the gorget) that may appear black in some lighting.

Voice: The wings produce a distinct humming sound, but the birds often make a variety of soft to loud chitters and squeaks.

Behavior: Very territorial or at least aggressive. Both males and females will chase other hummingbirds as well as moths, bees, and small birds from areas where they are feeding. A single male may attempt to control a quarter acre of flower garden.

Attracting and feeding: Ruby-throats and other hummers come to colorful flower plantings, especially tubular red flowers such as cardinal flowers. Adults feed largely on nectar and will frequent nectar feeders (a mix of one part sugar to four parts water, boiled for safety, often is recommended). They also take many tiny insects and spiders, which are a major food of the growing young.

Range: Breeds from southern Canada to the Gulf of Mexico mostly east of the Great Plains. West of the Great Plains it is replaced by the virtually identical Black-chinned Hummingbird, in which the male has the back edge of the throat iridescent violet.

Anna's Hummingbird • *Calypte anna*

What to look for: This is the common resident hummingbird of the Pacific Coast. The 4-inch adults are green above and faintly grayish green below with a long, nearly straight bill. Males are unmistakable, with an iridescent rose-red crown and throat, the feathers at the outer edges of the throat slightly elongated. Females are duller but usually have single or small groups of red feathers on the throat.

Voice: A series of squeaks and chitters is given by the male. Flying birds often produce a distinct rattling sound.

Behavior: Aggressive and quarrelsome, birds of both sexes often fight at feeders or flowers. Likely to be found anywhere there are flowers, from high mountain ranges to desert bottoms and meadows.

Attracting and feeding: Like other hummers, Anna's Hummingbird soon locates red nectar feeders and flower gardens with red, tubular flowers. This species often occurs in large numbers at feeders.

Range: A breeding bird from British Columbia to southeastern Arizona, mostly west of the Sierras and avoiding the central deserts, Anna's Hummingbird remains in most of this area over the winter and is not a long-distance migrant.

Broad-tailed Hummingbird • *Selasphorus platycercus*

What to look for: This is the common large (4-inch) breeding hummingbird of the central and southern Rocky Mountains. Both sexes have long, straight bills. Males are bright green above, including the crown, with a broad green area on the flanks and a white belly. The throat is totally iridescent red. Females have the throat white (sometimes with tiny red feathers) and are distinctly buffy on the sides and on the lower belly.

Voice: Broad-tailed Hummingbirds produce the usual chitters and squeaks.

Behavior: Flying birds, especially males, produce a sharp "tinnng" sound with the wings, often sounding like a ricocheting bullet and carrying long distances.

Attracting and feeding: Though they come to feeders, Broad-tailed Hummingbirds commonly are found in mountain forests and meadows, feeding on a variety of flowers. Hummingbird feeders will attract some birds, often during migration.

Range: Breeding from Idaho southward into Arizona and from Nevada to Colorado, Broad-tailed Hummingbirds migrate to Central America in the autumn. In the northern Rocky Mountains the species is replaced by the smaller Calliope Hummingbird, in which the male's throat has elongated strips of violet to reddish violet feathers.

Red-headed Woodpecker • *Melanerpes erythrocephalus*

What to look for: A 9-inch tricolored woodpecker, the adults black on the back and outer parts of the wings, stark white on the rump and belly, and with large white patches on the wings, The head, nape, and throat are bright red; there is a narrow black line separating red from the white of the breast. Immatures are streaky brownish on the back, throat, and head until their first winter but have the white rump and wing patches of the adults.

Voice: A harsh, loud "kerr" or "kwerr" is given during the summer, along with a variety of rattles and harsher chirps.

Behavior: Still common in the southern and central U.S., Red-heads have become rare in the Northeast, where they are losing suitable nesting trees to European Starlings. Red-heads like open areas and often are seen on fence posts and power poles along country roads and in parks. They may form sizable colonies in suitable areas.

Attracting and feeding: Red-heads will come to suet feeders and also will take sunflower seeds and acorns from hanging feeders. Trees in which nesting holes may be dug must be present to maintain colonies near feeders.

Range: Breeding from the Canadian border south to the Gulf of Mexico over the eastern U.S. (including the Great Plains), Red-headed Woodpeckers are year-round residents from Missouri and Virginia south.

Acorn Woodpecker • *Melanerpes formicivorus*

What to look for: Acorn Woodpeckers are the southwestern version of the Red-headed Woodpecker. Adults are black above, streaky white below, with a white rump and large white patches at the bases of the primary wing feathers (white across the secondaries in the Red-head). The nape is black, there is a black circle around the base of the gray bill, and a wide white band runs from over the bill onto the white throat. The eye is bright white. Males have a totally red crown; females have a black area over the eyes and a small red spot further back.

Voice: The call is a loud, annoying "waka-waka-waka" repeated ad nauseum.

Behavior: Largely restricted to oak and oak/pine woodlands, acorns form the major diet of the birds. They are noted for storing acorns in holes pecked in granary trees, often near houses and roads.

Attracting and feeding: A gentle, colonial bird that comes to sunflower feeders and also suet. It may ignore humans only a few feet away, making it a delightful bird to observe.

Range: This is a Mexican and Central American woodpecker that occurs in the U.S. from western Texas across the Southwest to the Pacific Coast of Oregon and California.

Red-bellied Woodpecker • *Melanerpes carolinus*

What to look for: A 9-inch "ladder-backed" woodpecker in which the entire back and the folded wings are covered by narrow alternating black and white bands, the Red-bellied Woodpecker is recognizable by the pearly gray sides of the face extending over the bright black eye. The nape is bright red in both sexes, with the crown red in males and gray in females; there usually is a small yellow band over the base of the long black bill. The rump is white.

Voice: A loud, harsh "churr" given repeatedly, plus a loud series of "pips."

Behavior: An abundant woodpecker that frequents open forests and often is common near lakes. They have adapted well to humans and often nest in old trees near houses, unless forced out by more aggressive Red-heads. Though efficient at digging insects from trees, they also pluck insects from leaves, ants from the ground, and may even be seen hovering over seeding plants of various types.

Attracting and feeding: Red-bellied Woodpeckers will come to a variety of foods, including the usual suet blocks, peanut butter mixes, and sunflower feeders. An easy bird to attract and hold at feeders.

Range: This is a resident woodpecker from central Texas to Minnesota, east to the Atlantic. Often abundant in the central and southern parts of the range, northern populations may disappear after long periods of cold weather. The more western Golden-fronted and Gila Woodpeckers have yellow and gray, rather than bright red, napes.

Yellow-bellied Sapsucker • *Saphyrapicus varius*

What to look for: A moderately large (8 inches long), long-billed woodpecker with a broad white oblique wing bar visible in perched birds, a white rump, and a yellow breast with small black streaks on the flanks. The back is black with narrow transverse white lines. The nape is black, often mottled with white, and there are two white stripes on the face bordering a black stripe through the eye, the lower (malar) stripe connected to a broad black bib. The crown and chin are both bright red in males, while the chin is white in females. Immatures are browner, with the head pattern indistinct.

Voice: Sometimes gives a "churr-churr" call or soft mewing sounds. Like other woodpeckers, it can produce a variety of louder squeaks and chatters.

Behavior: Usually solitary or in small colonies, sapsuckers drill rows of shallow holes in living trees, feeding on the sap and the insects attracted to the sap.

Attracting and feeding: Yellow-bellied Sapsuckers are easily attracted to suet and peanut butter feeders as well as sunflower seeds and peanut hearts; some will come to fruit.

Range: Yellow-bellied Sapsuckers breed from Alaska through Canada southeast to the Great Lakes and New England. They winter from the southern states to the West Indies and Central America. In the Rocky Mountains is the Red-naped Sapsucker, which has a red-black-red crown and a red band over the black bib.

Downy Woodpecker • *Picoides pubescens*

What to look for: This very common small (6.5 inches long) black and white woodpecker has a tiny bill that is only about as long as the distance from the eye to the base of the bill. The center of the back is white, as are the outer tail feathers (which commonly have two or three short black bars). Typically the face is marked with two large and variable white patches surrounding a black patch that includes the eye. The crown and nape are black, males with a red spot at the back of the crown.

Voice: The usual call is a soft, high-pitched "pic" as well as a low whinny.

Behavior: Common yard birds, Downy Woodpeckers are territorial during most of the winter, when males may force females away from feeders. When mating season begins in late winter, pairs form and together may operate a territory containing a few favored drumming poles or branches.

Attracting and feeding: Downy Woodpeckers probably are the most commonly attracted woodpeckers, coming readily to suet blocks and peanut butter logs. They also take peanut hearts and other nuts.

Range: Downy Woodpeckers are resident over virtually all of the U. S. and Canada, migrating little unless winter food resources are low. The almost visually identical Hairy Woodpecker also is found over all this range but is a larger bird (9 inches) with a bill that is distinctly longer than the distance from the eye to the base of the bill.

Northern Flicker • *Colaptes auratus*

What to look for: Northern Flickers are large (a foot long), very long-billed woodpeckers with brown- and black-barred backs and wings and a large white rump patch. Both sexes have grayish white underparts sprinkled with black dots and have a wide black bib below a gray throat. Birds from west of the Great Plains have rosy red underwings ("Red-shafted Flickers") while those from further east have bright yellow underwings ("Yellow-shafted Flickers"); the two forms are treated as subspecies groups. Male "Yellow-shafts" have a black malar stripe and a narrow red crescent on the nape; male "Red-shafts" have a bright red malar stripe; females of both forms have malar stripes weakly distinct from the facial color.

Voice: Northern Flickers often give a long series of loud "wick-wick-wick" calls that carry far and may sound like laughter. They also produce "kleer-a" notes when threatened.

Behavior: Though well-equipped for drilling into wood, Northern Flickers are ground-feeders that are seen hopping about in open areas feeding on ants and other small insects.

Attracting and feeding: Like other woodpeckers, Northern Flickers learn to come to suet and peanut butter feeders; some also take nuts and seeds. Try mealworms as a treat.

Range: Northern Flickers are found over the entire U.S. and Canada into tropical America. In southern Arizona and western Mexico also occurs the similar Gilded Flicker, once considered a subspecies. This flicker has yellow underwings and a bright red malar stripe in a pale gray face in males.

Black Phoebe • *Sayornis nigricans*

What to look for: A small (6.5 inches), stout, big-headed bird with a thin bill. The entire head, back, throat, breast, wings, and tail are black, a bit browner in young and worn plumage adults. The belly and undertail coverts are stark white.

Voice: Gives a pair of soft "pi-tsee" or "pee-wee" notes that rise and then drop.

Behavior: A bird of water in dry areas, Black Phoebes usually are seen perched on low branches, suddenly darting out after small insects. Courting males sing in flight while rising to heights, hovering, and then dropping. It often hovers just over the surface of the water. Pumps the tail up and down.

Attracting and feeding: Because the food consists almost exclusively of insects, Black Phoebes seldom come to feeders. They are easily attracted to large water baths and puddles during dry seasons.

Range: Black Phoebes are tropical American birds (found south to Argentina) that reach the northern part of their range in the U.S. Southwest, where they may occur all year from California to western Texas. In the southwestern Say's Phoebe the belly is tawny.

Eastern Phoebe • *Sayornis phoebe*

What to look for: A small (7 inches or less), rather big-headed dark gray and whitish flycatcher with a slender black bill, the Eastern Phoebe has the head, face, back, wings, and tail dark gray (the wings and tail almost black), the underparts white from the chin to the undertail coverts; the belly may be pale yellow in autumn, and there may be traces of an indistinct grayish band across the breast in some birds. The lack of wing bars and overall darker coloration help distinguish the Eastern Phoebe from other small eastern U.S. flycatchers.

Voice: The call usually is a simple two-syllable "fe-bee," accented on the "fe." To many birders the call sounds more like "pe-wee" and could be confused with that of the Eastern Wood-Pewee, which usually has a three-syllable call ("pe-a-wee").

Behavior: Though often found near water, Eastern Phoebes occur at the edges of many types of woodland and pasture areas, sitting on exposed branches and waiting for insects to venture close enough to chase. At rest, they pump the tail up and down and spread the feathers.

Attracting and feeding: Like other phoebes the food consists largely of insects, but during hard winters they may be forced to eat small seeds and berries and may be attracted to sunflower hearts and even suet.

Range: Found from the Great Plains eastward, Eastern Phoebes breed from central Canada to central Texas and Virginia. They migrate southward in winter, when they may be common in the Gulf states.

Ash-throated Flycatcher • *Myiarchus cinerascens*

What to look for: A relatively slender 8-inch flycatcher with a pair of weakly defined wing bars and bright rufous over the tail and in the primaries of the wings. The head and back are grayish brown to ashy brown, the low, rough crest not distinctly darker than the back. The underparts are pale, the throat and breast very pale gray, merging indistinctly into pale yellow belly and undertail coverts. The bill is uniformly blackish.

Voice: Usually Ash-throated Flycatchers can be recognized best by their loud "prrt," "ha-weer," and softer "ka-brick" calls. They are noisy birds calling from exposed perches.

Behavior: Abundant birds in parks and open woodlands, Ash-throated Flycatchers can be seen defending old woodpecker holes in trees and poles that serve as their nests. They may hawk for insects as well as pick ants and beetles off the ground.

Attracting and feeding: These insect-eaters may take sunflower and peanut hearts.

Range: Common from Oregon to central Texas during the breeding season, the Ash-throated Flycatcher spends the winter in Central America. In the eastern U.S. it is replaced by the Great Crested Flycatcher, a stouter, darker olive-brown bird with a bright yellow belly sharply demarked from the grayish chest and with different calls. Other very similar flycatchers occur in the southwestern U.S.

Western Kingbird • *Tyrannus verticalis*

What to look for: This fairly heavy-set 9-inch flycatcher has a pearly gray head and chest, bright yellow belly and undertail coverts, and blackish wings and tail. There are no wing bars in adult birds and at most a trace of a dark stripe through the eye to the rather short, heavy black bill. The outer tail feathers are narrowly edged with white.

Voice: Distinctive among related flycatchers, the Western Kingbird gives a loud one-syllable "whit" call, often repeated to distraction.

Behavior: Western Kingbirds often perch on fences and power lines along roads and in parks, waiting to fly out after insects. They often are seen hovering.

Attracting and feeding: Though they eat mostly insects, during dry periods with little prey they may take berries and thus can come to feeders. They are attracted to water.

Range: An abundant nesting bird from the Great Plains to the Pacific Coast, southern Canada to the Mexican border, the Western Kingbird leaves the country in the autumn to winter south to Costa Rica. Three other very similar kingbird species occur in the Southwest.

Eastern Kingbird • *Tyrannus tyrannus*

What to look for: A starkly black and white 8- to 9-inch flycatcher with a short, wide bill and at best traces of a pair of pale wing bars, Eastern Kingbirds are easily recognized by the broad white band across the end of the tail. The head, back, wings, and tail are black, the underparts from chin to undertail coverts white, sometimes with traces of a grayish band across the breast. Eastern Phoebes are never as black and white, are smaller, lack the white at the end of the tail, and pump the tail.

Voice: Sometimes gives a series of loud "kip-kip-kip" or "dzee-dzee-dzee" notes.

Behavior: Aggressive little birds noted for chasing hawks and crows, Eastern Kingbirds usually are seen flying from a hidden perch in a tree in pursuit of insects.

Attracting and feeding: Insect-eaters, Eastern Kingbirds seldom use feeders. They are fond of bees and often congregate near hives.

Range: Common breeding birds over most of the U.S. and Canada except the southwestern and Pacific Coast states, Eastern Kingbirds migrate to northwestern South America for the winter.

Blue Jay • *Cyanocitta cristata*

What to look for: Blue Jays are among our largest (11 inches) and most colorful (bright blue above, white to grayish white below) backyard birds, and they even have a high crest to make them more distinctive. The blue back is virtually unmarked, but the wings have a black and white pattern, while the top of the tail is narrowly banded with black and there are broad white edges to the tail. The face is white to grayish white, edged by a broken narrow black band that runs from the base of the blue crest to a narrow black bib.

Voice: Blue Jays mimic other birds and announce their presence with a loud "jay-jay-jay" or "thf-thf-thf," but they also have a "tweedle" whistle and a very liquid-sounding note like a tapped bell.

Behavior: Blue Jays are aggressive, conspicuous birds that feed on a variety of foods, from seeds and fruit to insects, and will rob nests to take eggs and hatchlings. Blue Jays will chase crows and hawks and often are chased by chickadees and other small birds.

Attracting and feeding: Blue Jays seem to especially love peanuts and sunflower seeds.

Range: Found from central Canada south to central Texas from the Atlantic Coast to the base of the Rocky Mountains, Blue Jays are resident in all but the most northern parts of the range. In the autumn, however, large migrant flocks form that move relatively short distances either north or south. From the Rocky Mountains to the Pacific Coast they are replaced by Steller's Jay, which is uniformly deep blue-black (usually fully black on the head and front third of the body) above and below except for small white spots near the eyes.

Western Scrub-Jay • *Aphelocoma californica*

What to look for: An 11-inch crestless jay that is deep blue above from the crown to the tail, with few markings except a narrow white stripe above each eye. The belly is white to grayish white, usually contrasting with a whiter throat and a breast that has sparse darker streaks. A narrow broken dark band (necklace) often separates the throat and breast color. The details of coloration and pattern vary greatly over its range.

Voice: The voice is loud, with a variety of calls including "shreep," "ike-ike," and "quick" variously joined and repeated. Often just squawks and makes assorted noises.

Behavior: Somewhat shyer than the Blue Jay, Western Scrub-Jays may form small foraging flocks that scour the ground and low vegetation for seeds, fruits, insects, and anything else edible.

Attracting and feeding: They will come to almost any type of feeder as well as puddles of water. They take anything, including peanuts and sunflower seeds, and may become nuisances, attacking smaller birds.

Range: Western Scrub-Jays are year-round residents from central Texas to the Pacific Coast, north to Colorado and Washington and south into Mexico. The larger Island Scrub-Jay is restricted to Santa Cruz Island off California, while the gray-backed Florida Scrub-Jay is restricted to central Florida.

Black-billed Magpie • *Pica pica*

What to look for: A Black-billed Magpie is almost 20 inches (half of this tail) of noisy, aggressive jay. The entire upper parts are black with strong blue and green tints; there is a broad white stripe across the wing. The throat and breast are black, as are the undertail coverts, but the belly is bright white. The bill is black, and there is no noticeable facial pattern. In flight there is a large white patch in each wing and a pair of broad white bands on the back extending to a pale rump; the central tail feathers are longest.

Voice: Loud and noisy like most other jays, Black-billed Magpies produce a variable series of "mag," "shak," and "chunk" notes.

Behavior: Black-billed Magpies form large flocks in farmlands and parks and have repeatedly been accused of raiding crops. Normally they feed heavily on insects of all types, but they do take some fruit and seeds and will raid nests of smaller birds.

Attracting and feeding: Like crows, Black-billed Magpies will come to feeders when it becomes hard to find natural foods, but they frighten off or attack smaller birds and usually are not desired.

Range: In North America, Black-billed Magpies are found from the Great Plains to northern Texas and west almost to the moist coniferous forests of the Pacific Coast. The species also is found in western Canada and Alaska, and the same species is found through most of northern Europe and Asia. The Yellow-billed Magpie of central California is virtually identical but has a yellow bill and yellow skin patches on the face.

Purple Martin • *Progne subis*

What to look for: A very large (8 inches) swallow with a forked tail and wings that do not extend beyond the tail. Adult males are glossy blue-black above and below with no pale features. Females and young males are brownish to grayish black with at least a small whitish area on the belly. The European Starling has shorter and more triangular wings and a much shorter, unforked tail, as well as a much longer bill.

Voice: A vocal swallow with a complicated repertoire, including a very liquid, bubbly song comprising twittering and "suw-weeh-weeh" in ascending and descending variations. In colonies there is much loud, cacophonous chatter.

Behavior: Seen flying in large and small groups, often flapping the wings when low but also soaring on fixed wings to higher altitudes. A very colonial bird, it once nested mostly in hollow trees near water, but today it is more likely to be found in groups of nesting boxes (often resembling hollowed gourds) fixed some 8 to 15 feet above the ground.

Attracting and feeding: Like other swallows, unlikely to come to feeders but will adopt nesting boxes if properly placed. Large colonies may form in boxes at one home while ignoring seemingly identical boxes just a few hundred yards away.

Range: Purple Martins appear over most of the eastern U.S. early in the spring and leave for South America early in autumn. Though the species occurs in the western U.S., it is not uniformly distributed there.

Tree Swallow • *Tachycineta bicolor*

What to look for: A slender, 5- to 6-inch swallow with very long wings extending well beyond the tail, which is shallowly forked. Both sexes are brilliant blue above with iridescent green tones and glossy white below. The white of the throat extends up almost to the eye and does not form a forward-curling point behind the eye. In flight, the white of the belly is barely visible on either side of the rump. Immatures are duller gray-brown above.

Voice: Sings on both the wing and at rest, producing a bubbly "ke-leet" and assorted twitters.

Behavior: Tree Swallows still prefer to nest in hollow trees in and near standing water such as lakes and ponds, often forming gigantic colonies. They fly rapidly with quick flaps of the wing but also glide efficiently. Immatures gain the full adult coloration by mid-autumn.

Attracting and feeding: Tree Swallows do not normally come to feeders and are more likely to be attracted to nest boxes placed near water.

Range: A breeding bird across the northern half of the U.S. plus Canada and Alaska to the Arctic Circle, Tree Swallows often do not migrate back to Central America until November and not uncommonly are still in the southern states in December. In the western U.S. and Canada the Violet-green Swallow is very similar but averages a bit smaller and has the white on the face extending in a pointed curve behind and above the eye; the belly color also extends up to leave only a narrow strip of blue-green on the rump.

Barn Swallow • *Hirundo rustica*

What to look for: A slender 6- to 7-inch swallow with a very deeply forked tail even in young and with a pair of long streamers in adults. Adults are bright blue above and buffy cinnamon below, with a deep rusty red throat bordered behind by a broken black line. Juveniles are paler below, white with a buffy throat. The underside of the tail is mostly white.

Voice: When flying, often gives an assortment of "sip" and "wip" notes.

Behavior: This abundant swallow hawks for insects over pastures, roadsides, meadows, and large lawns especially early and late in the day, sometimes forming large groups of adults and young. The cup-shaped mud and straw nests may be present in large numbers under bridges and in old farm buildings.

Attracting and feeding: Barn Swallows appear naturally where there are suitable open expanses for feeding and structures for placing nests.

Range: Barn Swallows are found virtually everywhere in North America during the spring to autumn, migrating to South America for the winter.

Black-capped Chickadee • *Poecile atricapillus*

What to look for: Among our most familiar birds, Black-capped Chickadees are very small (5 inches), very active mites. The back, wings, and tail are frosty gray, the crown and nape glossy black; a broad black bib extends from the chin to the upper breast. The lower half of the face and the underparts are white, often distinctly tinted with cinnamon in winter plumage. The lower edge of the bib is ragged, and the edges of many wing feathers are distinctly white.

Voice: Gives a low but harsh and slow "chick-a-dee-dee-dee" that is the most familiar call. The whistled call is usually given as a two- or three-syllabled "fee-bee-bee."

Behavior: Common to abundant in many types of forests, Black-capped Chickadees are loud, gentle, very visible birds that show little fear of humans. They feed mostly on the seeds of pines and other conifers but also take other seeds and fruits. During the winter they form mixed species feeding flocks. The nest is placed in a hole in a tree, often under a piece of loose bark.

Attracting and feeding: Black-capped Chickadees are abundant feeder birds. They take a variety of seeds as well as suet and peanut butter mixes but seem to prefer sunflower seeds, which are taken one at a time, flown away from the feeder, bashed on a hard object until broken, and the heart eaten.

Range: The Black-capped Chickadee is found from Alaska across Canada and the northern third of the United States, roughly north of a line from northern California to New Jersey. Six other species of chickadees are present in North America, all very similar but with more or less discrete ranges.

43

Carolina Chickadee • *Poecile carolinensis*

What to look for: Basically this is a southern version of the Black-capped Chickadee that is difficult to distinguish where the two species overlap in range; they sometimes hybridize. As a rule, Carolina Chickadees are a bit smaller and lighter in build than Black-caps and have the lower edge of the bib even rather than ragged. There seldom are distinct white edges to many of the wing feathers. Their voices also differ.

Voice: The call is like the Black-cap's, "chick-a-dee-dee-dee," but is higher pitched and given faster. The whistled call often is of four syllables, "fee-bee, fee-bay." The differences are not always obvious.

Behavior: Similar to that of the Black-capped. It often is found near cypress swamps and in pinelands.

Attracting and feeding: Like the Blacked-capped, it takes many types of seeds and will fly away with individual sunflower seeds.

Range: Southern U.S. from central Texas to southern Illinois and central New Jersey. There is little or no migration but some local movement.

Mountain Chickadee • *Poecile gambeli*

What to look for: This is the common resident chickadee of the Rocky Mountains and the interior deserts of the West. Adults are about 5 inches long and look much like a Black-capped Chickadee, being gray above and whitish below (sometimes with buffy tints), with a relatively small black bib, black crown, and white face. However, there is a narrow white stripe over the eye and the flanks tend to be distinctly gray.

Voice: The call is a rather hoarse version of the typical chickadee call, sometimes given as "chick-adee-adee-adee." The whistled call is the usual "fee-bee, fee-bay," but lower on the last notes.

Behavior: A bird of coniferous forests in the mountains and at the edge of valley parks, it nests in tree holes and sometimes can be seen looking from the hole, when the white eye stripes may be conspicuous.

Attracting and feeding: Similar to the other chickadees, again preferring sunflower seeds when available.

Range: A resident bird of the Rocky Mountains of the western U.S. and Canada, south to central Arizona and New Mexico, but not west to the wetter Pacific Coast. Common but sparsely distributed.

Chestnut-backed Chickadee • *Poecile rufescens*

What to look for: Probably the most distinctive chickadee, the Chestnut-backed appears relatively dingy at first glance. The crown and nape are black with brown tinges, the face is white, and there is a small black, ragged bib. The back and often the sides are bright to dingy rufous or cinnamon brown, but the tail and wings are blackish. The underparts are dirty white to grayish. The feathers of the wings often are strongly edged with white. The color of the back will distinguish it from other North American chickadees at a glance.

Voice: Harsh and penetrating, the call usually is along the lines of "tzek-a-zee-zee," but often only the "zee-zee" notes are given. The whistled note often is just "chek-chek."

Behavior: Just as active and gentle as the other chickadees, this species prefers wet coniferous forests in the northern part of the range and drier eucalyptus stands in the south. (Eucalyptus is of course introduced to the West Coast.) In keeping with the nature of western forests, this chickadee usually feeds high in the trees, but feeding flocks may haunt low shrubs.

Attracting and feeding: Chestnut-backed Chickadees come to backyard feeders like other chickadees and exhibit much the same feeding behaviors and preferences.

Range: Most populations are found along the Pacific Coast from southern Alaska to central California, but the species also lives in northern Idaho and adjacent areas.

Tufted Titmouse • *Baeolophus bicolor*

What to look for: Slightly larger than a chickadee (to 6 inches), Tufted Titmice also are small, active gray and white birds but with crests. The upper parts from the forehead to the tail are uniformly pale gray, usually with a small black patch just above the base of the bill. The crest is pointed, low but distinct, and often is raised when the bird is disturbed; from central Texas south and west it may be black, contrasting with the nape ("Black-crested Titmouse," usually treated as a subspecies). The eye is large, black, and very distinct in the pale grayish white face. The underparts are white, often weakly or strongly tinged with rufous.

Voice: The typical song is a loud whistle that commonly sounds like "peter-peter-peter" but is quite variable. It scolds with a variety of loud chatter observers who come too close.

Behavior: This abundant little bird associates with chickadees and other small birds most of the year but becomes more reclusive after forming breeding pairs. The eggs are placed in a hole in a tree, often an abandoned woodpecker nest. Like chickadees, it takes a variety of small insects and spiders along with what seeds are available. During the winter it may feed mostly on acorns.

Attracting and feeding: Tufted Titmice frequent feeders all year, taking a variety of seeds and also suet and peanut butter. They feed on sunflowers seeds like chickadees.

Range: A common to abundant bird over the entire eastern U.S., from the Great Lakes and New England to southern Texas. To the west it is replaced by the Oak and Juniper Titmice, which are similar but have smaller crests, grayer underparts lacking rufous tints, and lack black on the forehead or crest.

Bushtit • *Psaltriparus minimus*

What to look for: Bushtits are truly tiny (3.5 to 4 inches long) birds of slight build with long, floppy tails. The bill is very small, often hard to see without binoculars. The back, wings, and tail are pale to dark gray, the underparts grayish white sometimes with pale cinnamon tints on the flanks. Depending on subspecies and locale, some birds may have gray or brown crowns, pale brown or black faces; females have glassy yellow eyes, males black eyes. Pale wing bars are absent.

Voice: A constant chatter of soft contact notes, "tseet" and similar sounds.

Behavior: Most of the year is spent in large feeding flocks that move rapidly from shrub to shrub in deserts and dry prairies, often accompanied by other small bird species. The flight is weak and jerky. The nest is a surprisingly complicated hanging structure much like a small oriole's nest.

Attracting and feeding: Bushtits may come to feeders along with other small birds, taking a variety of seeds, including sunflower hearts. In natural situations they feed largely on small insects and spiders. Water will attract this species.

Range: A common year-long resident of the Southwest, it is found from the Pacific Northwest to central Texas into Mexico and Central America. In the southern part of its range it occurs with the Verdin, a similarly tiny bird that in the adult has a bright yellow head and throat and small reddish patches on the shoulders.

Red-breasted Nuthatch • *Sitta canadensis*

What to look for: A small (4 to 5 inches) forest bird with a sharply chiseled bill and overall blue-gray upper parts except for a black crown and nape. The face is white, with a broad black stripe running from the base of the bill through the eye toward the nape. Underparts are pale yellowish to bright rufous, darker toward the vent.

Voice: A series of slow, very nasal "nyak-nyak-nyak" notes, becoming faster and louder when the bird is annoyed. Often compared to a small toy tin trumpet.

Behavior: Nuthatches move much like tiny woodpeckers, going up and down branches and trunks, often head-down, searching for spiders and insects and using the bill to wedge out the prey. Red-breasted Nuthatches nest in coniferous forests and tend to feed on the small outer branches of trees. They join mixed species flocks in the winter.

Attracting and feeding: In the winter it comes to suet and peanut butter feeders and also takes sunflower seeds and other common feeder offerings.

Range: Red-breasted Nuthatches breed from Alaska across southern Canada to the northeastern U.S. and also at elevations in the Rocky Mountains. In the winter they may be found almost anywhere in the southern and central U.S.

45

White-breasted Nuthatch • *Sitta carolinensis*

What to look for: This 6-inch nuthatch has a relatively long bill and a stark contrast between a solid white face extending above the eye and a black crown and nape. The back and tail are blue-gray, often with white edges to the feathers, while the underparts are white; the vent often is strongly tinged with red.

Voice: A loud, nasal "yank-yank-yank" that is distinctive once heard.

Behavior: White-breasted Nuthatches frequent wetter mixed deciduous forests, often with many oaks and maples, but they also occur in pines and other conifers in the South and West. They hunt for insects on both branches and trunks of trees, moving rapidly often with the head down. Like other small birds, they often join mixed species flocks.

Attracting and feeding: White-breasted Nuthatches are common feeder birds in the winter, when the diet preference changes to fruits and seeds from the insects favored the rest of the year. They will feed at suet cages and also take peanut butter mixes.

Range: White-breasted Nuthatches are found in woodlands over much of the United States and southern Canada into Mexico, though they are found only in winter in southern Texas and along the Gulf of Mexico. Two much smaller white-faced nuthatches occur in the South and West, the Brown-headed and Pygmy Nuthatches respectively; these species have brown crowns and napes.

Brown Creeper • *Certhia americana*

What to look for: At first glance this small (5 inches), rather chunky woodpecker-like bird appears to be just streaked with brown and white above and is white below, but on closer examination it will be noticed that there is a distinct white line over the eye and the bill is long, slender, and slightly curved. The tail feathers are rufous and are spread so the individual spiny tips are visible, helping stabilize the bird on the trunk of a tree.

Voice: A soft "tseet" or "see" that does not carry far and is very high-pitched.

Behavior: Brown Creepers use their slender bills to probe holes and crevices in tree trunks for tiny insects, but they also take seeds during the winter. The feeding behavior is characteristic: the bird lands at the base of a tree and spirals upward, using the spiny tail feathers for support; when it reaches the top of the tree it flies down to the base of the next tree and starts over. Brown Creepers often join mixed species flocks in the winter.

Attracting and feeding: During the winter Brown Creepers may be attracted to hanging suet feeders and peanut butter mixes smeared on branches.

Range: Though the breeding range is largely restricted to coniferous forests from southern Canada into the northern United States and higher elevations such as the Rocky Mountains, in the winter Brown Creepers may be found anywhere in the United States.

Cactus Wren • *Campylorhynchus brunneicapillus*

What to look for: A 7- to 8.5-inch songbird recognizable as a wren by the slender, slightly curved bill, short wings, and the long and "floppy" tail carried loosely or held cocked over the back. The head is large, the body stout. The back is brown with many white streaks and spots, the wings are heavily marked with white, and the tail is barred with black above and spotted with white below. There is a rusty brown crown bordered below by a white eye brow stripe; an indistinct brown stripe forms the lower edge of this white stripe. The underparts are whitish grading to yellowish on the belly, heavily streaked with small dark brown lines; an indistinct brown bib sometimes is present.

Voice: A loud but hoarse and monotonous "chou-chou-chou-chou" to "cha-cha-cha-cha," reminiscent of a car refusing to start. Males often sing from exposed perches, the tail hanging straight down, the head up. Both sexes growl.

Behavior: The Cactus Wren usually feeds on or near the ground, often scratching through leaves for insects, seeds, and fruits; non-animal foods make up almost a quarter of the diet. The bulky nest of twigs and grasses may be well over a foot in diameter and is reached through a narrow passage; it is hung in chollas and spiny shrubs and is used as a roost all year. A pair maintains a territory often centering on the nest.

Attracting and feeding: Cactus wrens learn to come to seeds and cracked corn spread on or near the ground and may take suet and peanut butter. They also come to water.

Range: An abundant and characteristic bird of the southwestern deserts from central Texas to southeastern California into Mexico.

Carolina Wren • *Thryothorus ludovicianus*

What to look for: The largest wren in the eastern U.S. (to 6 inches long), the Carolina Wren is bright rusty brown above and pale buffy cinnamon below. The wings commonly have rows of small white spots, but the edges of the tail lack conspicuous white. There is a broad bright white eye brow stripe. The bill is long, slender, and slightly curved.

Voice: A loud, musical, and attractive variation on three syllables, "cheery-cheery-cheery" or "teakettle-teakettle-teakettle." The intensity and regularity of the song are more recognizable than the interpretation of the notes. Scolds, hisses, and chatters.

Behavior: A common wren that likes to call from hidden perches in open woodland and the edges of woods. It jerks the tail over the back like most other wrens.

Attracting and feeding: Though the diet consists mostly of insects, Carolina Wrens often visit feeding stations and come to birdbaths.

Range: Common over the eastern U.S. from central Texas to the southern Great Lakes and southern New England. Bewick's Wren, found from central Texas to the Pacific Coast (and once in the southern Appalachians but now apparently nearly extirpated there), is like a dull Carolina Wren with white barring or mottling on tail edges, brown to gray back, and whitish underparts.

House Wren • *Troglodytes aedon*

What to look for: A small (about 5 inches long), compact wren with a short tail that always appears longer than the length of the head. The bill is rather short and slender, slightly curved. The back is uniformly brown or nearly so, the wings and tail weakly striped with black. There is a faintly defined pale (buffy) eye ring and eye brow stripe in most birds. The underparts are dirty white under the throat to pale buff on the flanks, often with weak dark barring on the flanks and undertail coverts. Young birds may have a scaly pattern under the throat, while adults from southeastern Arizona may have distinctly brown-tinted throats ("Brown-throated Wren," usually considered a subspecies).

Voice: Hard to describe, a long, liquid but nasal and bubbly whistle with many ascending and descending parts. Males commonly call from exposed perches, often at heights, with the tail angled straight down and the head held up.

Behavior: Probably the most familiar North American wren, the House Wren often is found in back yards and around gardens and buildings. It scolds intruders and will chase larger birds and even cats as it defends its territory. House Wrens are noted for building their grassy nests in anything resembling a tree hole.

Attracting and feeding: House Wrens will take suet and other fatty feeds. They also use birdbaths.

Range: House Wrens are breeding birds through all the U.S. and southern Canada except the Gulf Coast states, where they occur as winter birds. Some may overwinter in the northern states, but many migrate to the tropics.

Golden-crowned Kinglet • *Regulus satrapa*

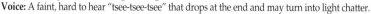

What to look for: Both kinglets in North America are very small (4 inches), rather chubby, large-headed, tiny-billed, big-eyed birds with slightly forked tails. A pair of white wing bars is present in the wing, the front bar weak, the longer posterior bar followed by a distinct blackish square and yellow feather edges. Golden-crowned Kinglets are greenish (with olive to grayish tones) above, white below, with a strongly contrasting head pattern of a broad white stripe through the eye bordered above by the black edges of the crown; a weaker dark stripe is below the white stripe. The black crown has a large yellow spot or stripe in both sexes, but in males the center of the yellow spot becomes bright orange.

Voice: A faint, hard to hear "tsee-tsee-tsee" that drops at the end and may turn into light chatter.

Behavior: Active little birds that often hover while searching branches and leaves for insects and spiders, Golden-crowned Kinglets commonly are members of mixed species flocks in the winter. They have a habit of nervously twitching the wings even while resting on a perch.

Attracting and feeding: Like many other small birds, Golden-crowned Kinglets come to feeders during cold winter weather and will take suet and other fatty foods. They also will use sheltering bushes near feeders.

Range: Golden-crowned Kinglets breed in cool northern coniferous forests from Alaska and Canada to the northeastern U.S. and at high elevations in the eastern and western mountains. During the winter they migrate as far south as Guatemala, but they may be common winter birds throughout the U.S.

47

Ruby-crowned Kinglet • *Regulus calendula*

What to look for: Similar in size and form to the Golden-crowned Kinglet, the Ruby-crowned appears uniformly olive-green to grayish green above with white underparts that usually are distinctly buffy to yellowish on the belly. The black eye is set in a strongly contrasting white oval that usually forms a ring slightly broken above and below the eye. The crown feathers of the male have red bases.

Voice: A high-pitched, hard to hear "tseet-tseet-tseet" sometimes varied with "jee-tit" notes. Also chatters.

Behavior: A nervous, active little bird that repeatedly twitches the wings even when at rest. It constantly appears to be searching for small insects as food and may hover over leaves.

Attracting and feeding: May be very abundant during winter in the U.S. and come to feeders with other small birds. They will hang on suet bells and chip at peanut butter mixes.

Range: Breeding in cool coniferous forests, Ruby-crowned Kinglets are found in summer from the Rocky Mountains to northern Alaska and across Canada to the Great Lakes area and northern New England. In the winter they migrate south as far as Guatemala and may be abundant across the southern half of the U.S.

Blue-gray Gnatcatcher • *Polioptila caerulea*

What to look for: Very small (a bit over 4 inches) but long-tailed and sleek birds with slender but strong bills, Blue-gray Gnatcatchers are indeed blue-gray above and white below. There are no wing bars. Both sexes have a distinct white eye ring that is complete, without breaks, and breeding males have a faint blackish line above the eye and a slightly darker blue-gray crown than in females. The tail is black above and white below, edged with white.

Voice: An ascending series of weak "tseet" or "pseet" notes forming a hard to hear buzzy song. Also chatters and has weak insect-like chips.

Behavior: Blue-gray Gnatcatchers are active searchers of leaves and branches for insects and spiders, foraging from near the ground in dense thickets to near the top of tall trees, constantly buzzing and chipping. They often cock the tail over the back and spread it to display the contrasting white and black feathers. The nest is a tiny cup covered with lichens and usually placed fairly conspicuously on a high branch.

Attracting and feeding: Though Blue-gray Gnatcatchers will visit feeders with other small birds, their insect diet means they seldom take seeds. They will visit suet blocks, however, and use the cover of nearby bushes.

Range: Blue-gray Gnatcatchers nest in forested areas across the central and southern U.S., except in the generally treeless Great Plains. In winter most migrate to the Caribbean islands and Central America.

American Robin • *Turdus migratorius*

What to look for: This is one of our larger backyard birds (10 to 11 inches long), often terrestrial, with an erect stance, yellow bill, and a long tail. The back is dark brown to nearly black; wing bars are absent. Females have dark gray heads, but males usually have contrasting black heads. There is an incomplete but very conspicuous white ring around the eye. The throat is white, often with narrow dark streaks, distinctly set off from the bright orange, brick red, or reddish clay breast and upper belly; the undertail coverts are white. Young birds have spotted breasts for a short while.

Voice: The cheery bird—the loud, variable song usually includes the phrases "cheery-cheerio-cheeriup" and variants intermixed with "tut" and "sip" notes.

Behavior: American Robins feed on a variety of foods, from berries and small fruits in the winter to the more common fare of insects and earthworms the rest of the year. They feed both individually and in tremendous flocks, from the ground to the tops of trees. The nest, often built in trees in backyards, usually has a ring of mud around the inside edge.

Attracting and feeding: In summer American Robins will come to birdbaths and also dust baths and will sometimes take peanut butter mixes, but they are not great seedeaters. In the winter, however, they take a variety of softer seeds and fruits. Try mealworms as a treat in the summer.

Range: As breeding birds, American Robins are abundant over the northern two-thirds of the U.S. and most of Canada and Alaska; they follow the mountains in the Southwest to the Mexican border. A few American Robins breed in the southern states, but there they are much more common in gigantic winter flocks.

Eastern Towhee • *Pipilo erythrophthalmus*

What to look for: Though smaller than an American Robin (7 to 8 inches long) and with a short, conical black bill, this ground-feeding bunting looks much like that bird. The entire head, throat, upper breast, and back, including the tail, are black (males) or brown (females), with traces of a broken white wing bar and some white edges to the primary wing feathers. The flanks are bright burnt orange, separated by a broad white stripe from the level of the legs to the dark throat; undertail coverts are pale yellow or buffy. The eyes are red in most specimens, though Florida birds may have staring white eyes. Young birds are buffy with brown streaks above and below.

Voice: The song usually is interpreted as "drink your tea-tea-tea" but can be greatly shortened to what sounds like "drink tea" or just "teeea."

Behavior: This is a skulker usually located by following its distinctive song or the sounds of scratching among dead leaves as the bird looks for insects and seeds.

Attracting and feeding: Eastern Towhees often come to feeders, taking small seeds and cracked corn near or on the ground. They also will feed on peanuts and sunflower seeds.

Range: This towhee can be found over much of the eastern U.S. to the Canadian border, and it is resident over the southeastern states. This species and the western Spotted Towhee (with distinct rows of white spots on the wings and upper back) formerly were combined as a single species, the Rufous-sided Towhee.

Eastern Bluebird • *Sialia sialis*

What to look for: A stout 7-inch thrush with a rather large head, the bill short but strong, the tail fairly long. Males are brilliant iridescent blue from the forehead to the tip of the tail. The face is bluish gray. The underparts from the chin to the breast are bright reddish orange, but the belly and undertail coverts are clean white. In females the colors are subdued and the head may be gray with a white eye ring visible; the throat is pale orange. Young birds are brown above with blue in the middle of the back and spotted breasts.

Voice: A loud and not especially musical series of notes based on "chur-chur-churlee."

Behavior: Eastern Bluebirds lay their eggs in holes in trees and posts, and today they have lost much nesting habitat to European Starlings. In many parts of the country they almost disappeared until given nest boxes situated at the edges of fields. The diet consists of many small invertebrates as well as berries and small seeds.

Attracting and feeding: Eastern Bluebirds are best attracted by providing nest boxes at the edges of pastures and meadows. They may take peanut hearts and raisins.

Range: Eastern Bluebirds are year-round residents from Oklahoma to Illinois and New Jersey south. Many leave the U.S. to winter as far south as Nicaragua. In the western U.S. it is replaced by the very similar Western Bluebird, which has a blue throat in males (gray in females). Mountain Bluebirds also are western and in males are blue above and below.

Northern Mockingbird • *Mimus polyglottos*

What to look for: A large (11 inches), relatively slender, long-tailed gray and white bird. Upper surfaces from the forehead to the base of the tail are uniformly gray, the wings and tail blackish. The wing has two narrow white bars and a large white spot at the elbow; the tail has white outer edges. The underparts are white, sometimes dingy; young birds have triangular dark spots over the throat and breast for a few years. The eyes are yellow, the bill black.

Voice: Accomplished mimics, Northern Mockingbirds sing a prolonged and highly variable song of original and mimicked phrases and also have a loud "tchik" contact note. They repeat each phrase three times or more in a row before changing phrase; Brown Thrashers seldom repeat a phrase more than two or three times.

Behavior: Northern Mockingbirds like to sing from high perches for hours at a time, day and night. They are aggressive, both sexes fighting their neighbors and intruders of any species, including cats, dogs, and humans.

Attracting and feeding: Northern Mockingbirds frequent feeders more to disturb other birds that may be within their territory than to vary their insect diet with seeds. They will take some suet, raisins, and other soft foods.

Range: A common to abundant permanent resident across the southern half of the U.S. from coast to coast, Northern Mockingbirds have extended their range northward in the East over the last decades, taking advantage of human development.

Brown Thrasher • *Toxostoma rufum*

What to look for: Similar to the Northern Mockingbird in size and shape, Brown Thrashers are bright rufous above and creamy to yellowish white below. There are two white wing bars and often an indistinct dark patch behind the eye; heavy brown streaking runs from the chin to the belly, but the undertail coverts are clean. The bill is slightly curved; the eye is yellow.

Voice: Brown Thrashers produce a variable song of many different phrases that usually are repeated only twice or occasionally three times before starting over. They have a loud, hard "spack" note and also a low growl.

Behavior: Brown Thrashers feed on and near the ground, often loudly scratching through dead leaves in thickets or picking insects from freshly watered lawns. They feed on insects, seeds, and small fruits. Their liking for dense cover may make them hard to observe, but they are not shy birds and will eventually come out for the patient birder.

Attracting and feeding: Their varied diet allows Brown Thrashers to winter in much of the southern half of the U.S., when they will come to feeders with peanuts, suet, and fruit. They also visit birdbaths and will dust bathe.

Range: Common across the eastern U.S. and southern Canada, including the Great Plains states, Brown Thrashers tend to migrate to the warmer states during colder winters, though a few may linger near feeders even in the Northeast. The Long-billed Thrasher of eastern Mexico ranges north into the lower Rio Grande valley of Texas; it has a grayer head and blacker streaking on the underparts, as well as a slightly longer, more curved bill.

Curve-billed Thrasher • *Toxostoma curvirostre*

What to look for: In size and shape the Curve-billed Thrasher is similar to a Northern Mockingbird but the bill is long and distinctly curved. The upper parts are faded brown, the tail sometimes darker; there may be two thin white wing bars. The underparts are dirty white to pale brown, usually mottled or finely spotted with brown that is heaviest on the breast; the throat commonly is white with a distinct narrow dark brown stripe on each side running to the base of the blackish bill. Undertail coverts are sandy brown, usually unmarked; the black underside of the tail ends in large white spots. The eye is yellow. Young birds have shorter, less curved bills.

Voice: Most often heard is a loud "whit-wheet" call that may be given from atop exposed perches. Males also produce a quite musical, lively, and varied song. Very vocal.

Behavior: This is an abundant bird of dry canyons, old pastures, and desert, where it often frequents cactus jumbles and spiny underbrush. It will eat almost any small invertebrate it finds and also takes small fruits and seeds. Active in the hottest weather, even at midday.

Attracting and feeding: Curve-billed Thrashers learn to come to feeders and take a variety of foods, from oranges to peanuts and suet. They are even easier to attract to dripping or slightly flowing water.

Range: A bird of the dry Southwest, it is found from southern Arizona to central Texas and into Mexico.

Cedar Waxwing • *Bombycilla cedrorum*

What to look for: Cedar Waxwings are 7-inch birds of stocky shape, with distinctive glossy warm brown heads with long, pointed brown crests. The head and back are uniformly brown, the rump gray, the tail black with a broad yellow band at its tip. The underparts are brown grading to bright yellow on the belly, the undertail coverts white. There are bright red waxy droplets at the ends of the secondary feathers of the wings, which also have a narrow white stripe on their inner edges. There is a black mask through the eye.

Voice: A soft "see-see-see-see" that carries quite well, especially when given by a large flock of birds. Commonly calls while in flight.

Behavior: Cedar Waxwings tend to move in flocks of dozens of birds searching for fruiting trees. Almost three-quarters of their diet consists of berries and small fruits, including juniper, holly, and myrtle berries, but they also take a few insects as well as nectar and sap.

Attracting and feeding: Raisins may attract Cedar Waxwings to feeders, especially if fruiting trees are in the area.

Range: Cedar Waxwings breed in North America from coast to coast from central Canada to the northern third of the U.S. In winter they migrate as far as South America and may appear anywhere in the U.S. Bohemian Waxwings, slightly larger and with red undertail coverts, breed from Alaska to western Canada and generally winter in the northwestern U.S., rarely being found in the Northeast.

Yellow Warbler • *Dendroica petechia*

What to look for: A 5-inch warbler with a thin black bill and a large black eye set in a yellow face. Though variable, as a rule the head and underparts are bright yellow in males, duller in females, with many narrow bright red or reddish brown streaks on the breast and upper belly of the male (rarely visible in females). The back is yellowish green in males to dull grayish green with yellow tints in immatures and some females. The wings and relatively short tail are darker, the edges of all the larger feathers yellowish; there are large yellow spots in the tail feathers visible in perched and flying birds.

Voice: The song is loud and easily recognizable: three similar syllables followed by three slightly different syllables, usually translated as "sweet-sweet-sweet, I'm so sweet."

Behavior: Yellow Warblers tend to be most common in moist areas, from trees and shrubs near lakes and rivers to alder thickets around wet meadows.

Attracting and feeding: Like other warblers, Yellows are insectivores and seldom come to feeders, though they have been known to take small mealworms and rarely suet. They will come to birdbaths.

Range: The most wide-ranging breeding North American warbler, found from northern Alaska south coast to coast from southern California to North Carolina and also in the Florida Keys (where males may have red crowns). The birds migrate to Central America as early as late July.

Yellow-rumped Warbler • *Dendroica coronata*

What to look for: Breeding males of this 5.5-inch warbler are dark blue-gray to black above with a yellow crown, a broad black bib, and heavy black streaking along the flanks, but females and winter adults look quite different. In all plumages, look for a large yellow patch on the rump in combination with a yellow spot or smudge on the side just below the bend of the wing. There are large white patches in the tail. Winter birds are streaky brownish above, white with narrow dark streaks below, the breast not heavily marked.

Voice: The song is a variation of a simple "tweet-tweet-tweet" that may rise or fall at the end. During the winter the birds produce a soft "cheet" and chatter.

Behavior: This is the only warbler likely to be found in much of the U.S. during the winter, sometimes being seen in large groups. They often join mixed species foraging flocks.

Attracting and feeding: Breeding birds seldom visit feeders though they may come to birdbaths. In winter, Yellow-rumps may come to feeders with other small birds and take suet and peanut butter.

Range: Yellow-rumped Warblers breed in cool coniferous forests from Alaska to the northeastern U.S. and at higher elevations in much of the western U.S., most migrating south to Central America and the West Indies. Some overwinter in the eastern and southwestern U.S. The Magnolia Warbler, found mostly east of the Great Plains, has a yellow breast and throat in all plumages in addition to a yellow rump and white tail spots.

Scarlet Tanager • *Piranga olivacea*

What to look for: A relatively heavy-bodied 7-inch songbird with a short but thick and slightly curved grayish bill. Breeding males are distinctive: brilliant scarlet red above and below, from crown to rump and undertail coverts, with glossy black wings and tail. Females and autumn males are uniformly olive-green above and yellowish below with a greenish tint; the wings are brown. There are no distinct wing bars.

Voice: A loud song of four or five syllables much like an American Robin's but coarser, often given as "queer-queer-queery-querry-queert." Also a loud "chip-burrr" note.

Behavior: Scarlet Tanagers, for all their bright colors, tend to stay in the upper parts of trees with dense leaf cover and are difficult to observe. They move slowly in search of insects and spiders. Males may call for long periods from a well-hidden perch.

Attracting and feeding: Scarlet Tanagers feed on insects but also take some fruit; they may visit oriole feeders and take some suet.

Range: Scarlet Tanagers breed in the eastern U.S. and southern Canada east of the Great Plains and south to Arkansas and the Carolinas. They winter as far south as Bolivia. Western Tanagers (west of the Great Plains) have two wingbars and look like a female Scarlet Tanager; males have red heads.

Vermilion Flycatcher • *Pyrocephalus rubinus*

What to look for: A small (6 inches), rather delicate phoebe-like flycatcher, the males resembling Scarlet Tanagers at first glance, but of course with the small, slender black bill of a flycatcher. Adult males are bright red from the chin to the undertail coverts, with a large bright red crest; the back, wings, tail, and a band through the eye are dark brown. Females and immatures are brownish above, white below with narrow brown streaks, the belly and undertail coverts yellowish to orange.

Voice: Relatively silent, but a three-syllable "peet-a-see" song and a "pseep" note are given.

Behavior: Often abundant in moist lowlands with shrubs and grasses. It acts much like a phoebe, including pumping the tail up and down and darting after insects, especially bees. Males court females by flying high and descending on fluttery wings.

Attracting and feeding: Seldom comes to feeders though it may be attracted to birdbaths and will even take some suet.

Range: A familiar summer bird of the southwestern U.S. from southern California and Nevada to central Texas, Vermilion Flycatchers have a tendency to wander during their migrations and sometimes appear in the eastern U.S. They are resident over much of tropical America as far south as Argentina.

American Tree Sparrow • *Spizella arborea*

What to look for: A 6-inch sparrow typically with a distinct black spot (the "stickpin") toward the center of the grayish white chest. The crown is rufous, contrasting with a gray head and nape; there is a broken dark line through the eye, turning into a rufous spot behind the eye. The wings have two white wing bars; there is a rufous wash on the flanks below the wings. The bill is bicolored: black above, yellow below. The tail is long, narrowly edged with white, and is slightly forked.

Voice: Typically quite musical, with the first two notes higher than the rest, plus a triple note, "tsee-deele-et" or the like.

Behavior: Seen in the winter in the U.S., it is a typical sparrow that may feed in large flocks in old fields and the edges of woods. Birds often perch in shrubs below eye level.

Attracting and feeding: American Tree Sparrows often come to feeders and will take small seeds and cracked corn spread near the ground.

Range: A breeding bird only in Alaska and extreme northern Canada, American Tree Sparrows may be abundant winter birds across the northern two-thirds of the U.S. east of the Rocky Mountains. During exceptionally cold winters they may be pushed south to the Gulf Coast. Females may winter further south than males. The Field Sparrow, an abundant breeding and winter resident throughout the eastern U.S., lacks the stickpin and has a bright pink bill.

Chipping Sparrow • *Spizella passerina*

What to look for: A small (about 5 to 5.5 inches), rather slightly built sparrow with a long, slightly forked tail. Adults have a bright rusty brown crown bordered below by a broad white line and then a narrow black stripe from the base of the bill through the eye toward the nape. The back and wings are streaky brownish; there are two broken white wing bars; the lower back and rump are distinctly gray. The underparts are clean grayish white. Winter birds have a less defined head pattern. The bill is uniformly colored.

Voice: A very fast trill or rattle at a single pitch—basically a long series of connected "chip" notes.

Behavior: Chipping Sparrows may be abundant on lawns and in pastures at the edge of woodlands. They are tame birds often seen in large flocks picking for seeds in old fields. Males sing persistently from exposed perches.

Attracting and feeding: Like other sparrows, Chipping Sparrows rapidly locate feeders and will come for small seeds. They often associate with other sparrows during the winter, especially at feeders.

Range: An abundant breeding bird over virtually all of North America except the dry southern Great Plains, Chipping Sparrows winter from the southernmost states to Central America. Clay-colored Sparrows, breeding in the northern U.S. and Canada, have duller crowns (with a narrow gray stripe through the center) and a distinct malar stripe running down from the base of the bill and bordered behind by white.

Fox Sparrow • *Passerella iliaca*

What to look for: Fox Sparrows appear larger and bulkier than their 7-inch length. The tail is long. Coloration is
very variable, but generally the birds are bright reddish brown to grayish brown
on the back, wings, and tail, lacking white wing bars. The breast and belly are
strongly streaked and spotted with bright reddish brown, sometimes setting off
a whiter throat. The face generally is uniformly grayish or brown, the crown and
nape typically gray. In many birds the breast streaking merges into a large,
irregular stickpin.

Voice: The song is a musical cluster of a variety of notes, beginning with a short
whistle.

Behavior: When noted, Fox Sparrows usually are found scratching through leaves and
litter inside dense thickets. They are secretive birds even when common. During the
winter large numbers may appear at the edges of woodlands and pastures.

Attracting and feeding: Fox Sparrows may be common at feeders in the winter, taking a
variety of seeds and other offerings. They stand out by their large size and dark coloration.

Range: Fox Sparrows breed across Alaska and northern Canada and at elevations across the northwestern
U.S. to central California. In winter they may be found almost anywhere in the U.S., especially in the
southeastern states. The many color forms (subspecies) often mingle during the winter. Harris's Sparrow (Great
Plains) has a black face and pinkish bill.

Song Sparrow • *Melospiza melodia*

What to look for: A fairly large (6 to over 7 inches long), long-tailed sparrow with just traces of white wing bars.
The tail is broadly rounded. Two elements of the streaky brown coloration are distinctive: a dark brown (almost
black) wedge-like malar stripe from the corners of the bill on either side of the white throat, and a large, irregular
brown stickpin on the breast. The brown crown is split by a gray stripe; there is heavy
streaking on the sides of the breast and belly.

Voice: One of the most easily learned songs for a sparrow: "sweet-sweet-sweet, buzz"
and a trill. Individuals may vary and leave out parts of the song or repeat others.

Behavior: Song Sparrows often are abundant birds forming breeding colonies in
dense shrubs and thickets at the edges of woods and pastures, often near water.
They feed both on the ground and in the vegetation. Males sing from exposed
perches. The flight is slow and weak, the birds usually pumping the long tail up and
down in flight.

Attracting and feeding: These birds come to feeders after any type of seed, from millet to
peanuts. Song Sparrows often take advantage of birdbaths and pools.

Range: The many subspecies of Song Sparrow breed coast to coast from across the central U.S. (California to
Virginia) and north through central Canada. In winter, Song Sparrows may be found anywhere in the U.S.

White-throated Sparrow • *Zonotrichia albicollis*

What to look for: A chunky, long-tailed 7-inch ground sparrow that always has a white throat sharply set off from
a darker breast. In adults the head has three wide white or buffy stripes (through the center of the crown and
from the base of the bill through the top of the eye to the nape) bordered by black. There is a bright
yellow spot in the lores (between the base of the bill and the eye). The lower sides of the face and
the breast are bright gray, the belly white; the clean white throat is outlined by a narrow
broken black line. Typically the bill is pale at the base; the tail is slightly notched. Juveniles
have a poorly defined head pattern and weak streaking on the breast.

Voice: The song is readily recognized, often heard as "old sam peabody-peabody-
peabody" or "pure sweet Canada-Canada-Canada."

Behavior: This is a characteristic winter bird in much of the eastern U.S., where
large flocks may form to scratch in leaves and litter for seeds and other foods.
They are one of the first winter migrants noticed and one of the last to leave
in the spring. The song is given throughout the year.

Attracting and feeding: Flocks of White-throated Sparrows often descend on feeders,
digging through the seeds dumped on the ground by other birds. Give them a low feeding table or seeds spread
on the ground.

Range: White-throated Sparrows breed across northern and central Canada and spend the winter in the eastern
and southern U.S. from New Mexico to New England. Some birds breed in the extreme northeastern U.S.

White-crowned Sparrow • *Zonotrichia leucophrys*

What to look for: Easily mistaken both in breeding plumage and in winter garb for the White-throated Sparrow, this is a 7-inch, long-tailed ground sparrow. Breeding birds have gray faces, napes, and breasts, with a poorly defined white throat and white to buffy belly and sides. There are three broad stark white stripes on the head, all bordered by strong black lines; a yellow lore spot is absent. The white throat is not outlined with black. The bill is yellow to pink. Immatures are brownish, streaked above and below, with a brown crown and face; there is a weak pale stripe through the center of the crown and a grayish stripe back from the eye. Immatures and winter adults have a characteristically high forehead, and immatures give the impression of having a crew-cut.

Voice: The song varies with range and subspecies, but usually it is a single whistled note.

Behavior: Often common, White-crowns usually are noticed scratching for seeds in the litter. They may form large flocks during the winter, often mixing with White-throats. Winter immatures may be difficult to distinguish from immature White-throats.

Attracting and feeding: White-crowns frequent feeders to scratch through the smaller seeds.

Range: White-crowned Sparrows are common to abundant breeding birds from Alaska and northern Canada into the mountains of northwestern U.S. They may be year-round residents in the western states, but during the winter they are found over the central and southern states from coast to coast and into Mexico.

Golden-crowned Sparrow • *Zonotrichia atricapilla*

What to look for: The Golden-crowned Sparrow is very similar to the White-throated Sparrow, including the long, slightly notched tail and white throat (which is weakly or not outlined with dark). The face may be gray to brown. Adults have a black crown with a broad bright yellow swatch through the center; there is no white outlining the crown stripe. The breast is buffy or gray, unstreaked in adults, streaked in immatures. Winter adults and many young (shown) have a streaky brown crown with a yellow spot.

Voice: This sparrow has been interpreted as calling out its name in three descending notes: "gol-den-crown." The song also is interpreted as "oh-dee-mee."

Behavior: Generally similar to White-throats, digging through litter in the winter. Breeding takes place in low shrubs and stunted trees at high elevations.

Attracting and feeding: Golden-crowned Sparrows may come to feeders in the winter, scratching through dropped seeds and feeding at low tables.

Range: Breeding populations occur from northern Alaska south almost to the U.S. border. Wintering birds are found along the Pacific Coast from British Columbia through California.

Dark-eyed Junco • *Junco hyemalis*

What to look for: In this 6-inch ground-feeding, flocking sparrow the head is dark, black to gray or brown, strongly contrasted to the pale yellow bill. The back is unstreaked in adults, the rump is gray or brown, and the tail is black with the outer tail feathers solid white. Wing bars are obvious in only one form. Juveniles are streaked on the head, back, and breast, but they still have a dark tail with white outer feathers. The eye is always black. Four basic color forms include: 1) The "Slate-colored Junco" is dark blackish gray (browner in females than males) over the entire upper parts, head, throat, and breast, with the belly a contrasting white. This is the common wintering bird in the eastern U.S. 2) "Oregon Juncos" have the head, throat, and breast black, contrasting to white underparts and a brown back. The sides are buffy. 3) "Pink-sided Juncos" are similar with a grayer head and breast less contrasted to the brown back; the sides are bright pinkish buffy. 4) "Gray-headed Juncos" are gray over the entire head and nape, the underparts, and the rump, black in front of the eyes, and bright reddish brown in the center of the back.

Voice: The song is a monotonous whistled note. Flocks have a soft twitter.

Behavior: Though these are ground-feeding sparrows, they seldom scratch through the leaves. Instead they hop about and rather delicately pick up small seeds on the surface.

Attracting and feeding: One of the most common winter feeder birds, Dark-eyed Juncos may be found at almost any feeder, looking for seeds on the ground.

Range: Dark-eyed Juncos breed across Alaska and Canada and are year-round residents in the mountains of both the western and eastern U.S.

Northern Cardinal • *Cardinalis cardinalis*

What to look for: The Northern Cardinal is one of the most familiar birds of the eastern U.S. It is a rather long-tailed 9-inch songbird with a tall, pointed crest at all ages and sexes. The bill is short and conical, the upper and lower halves about of equal size; it is bright orange in adults, grayish in young. Adult males are bright red overall except for a black patch around the base of the bill; the back, wings, and tail often are shaded with dusky brown. Females are dusky brown below and on the head, darker brown with strong red tones on the back, wings, and tail; young males are similar but have a red flush on the underparts.

Voice: Though it may have complicated songs, the most familiar song is a bright "cheer-cheer-cheer," loud, penetrating, and repeated for long periods. The loud "chip" also becomes recognizable with practice.

Behavior: An abundant bird found in wet and dry woodlands, yards, and roadsides, preferring dense cover but well-adapted to human environments. Northern Cardinals have strong pair bonds and are territorial; females sing. There may be as many as four broods of young a year, this accomplished by the male taking care of the young while the female is on the nest with the next clutch of eggs.

Attracting and feeding: Northern Cardinals feed on a variety of insects but also take many fruits and seeds, and they readily visit feeders to take sunflower seeds, peanut hearts, safflower, and many smaller seeds. One of the most common feeder birds in its range.

Range: Resident from the Great Plains and central Texas to the Canadian border and the Atlantic Coast, rarer in the Southwest and ranging into Mexico.

Summer Tanager • *Piranga rubra*

What to look for: A 7- to 8-inch songbird with a thick, slightly curved bill that is yellow during the breeding season and grayish the rest of the year. Breeding males are red (rosy to distinctly orange-tinged) from crown to rump and on the underparts, with browner wings and tail. Females and immatures are greenish yellow below, more olive on the back; young breeding males are like females with many reddish patches. Wing bars are absent.

Voice: The song is similar to the "cheer-cheery-cheer" song of the American Robin but hoarser, often interrupted with a "pit-tuck" note.

Behavior: Like other tanagers, Summer Tanagers are birds of deep forests, often near rivers and lakes, where they tend to slowly and deliberately hunt for insects high in trees. Calling males are difficult to locate even with their loud calls.

Attracting and feeding: Summer Tanagers often come to feeders in search of orange halves, suet, sugar water, and even peanuts.

Range: A breeding bird of the southern U.S. from southern California to central Texas and to the Atlantic Coast, north to Iowa and New Jersey, the Summer Tanager migrates to tropical America, south to Bolivia.

Pyrrhuloxia • *Cardinalis sinuatus*

What to look for: This Mexican version of the Northern Cardinal has a somewhat longer crest than that bird and a heavier, more yellowish bill in which the lower mandible is much deeper than the upper and distinctively curved. Overall coloration is grayish, paler on the underparts, with somewhat darker wings and tail. Males have a ragged red stripe from around the base of the bill down the center of the underparts, with red crest and wing feather edges. Females lack red except at the tip of the crest and sometimes on the breast. The wing linings are pinkish to rosy red, paler in females.

Voice: A rather higher pitched "cheer-cheer-cheer" song like that of the Northern Cardinal, plus a loud "chip" or "chink" note.

Behavior: Pyrrhuloxias are birds of thorn scrub, often seen perched on mesquites but also on power lines along rural roads. Males may twitch the tail and wings while singing. They look and act much like the more familiar Northern Cardinal.

Attracting and feeding: Like Northern Cardinals, Pyrrhuloxias visit feeders and take a variety of seeds, including peanuts and safflower. They also are easily attracted to water.

Range: Resident in the extreme southwestern U.S. from southeastern Arizona to south-central Texas and often common.

Rose-breasted Grosbeak • *Pheucticus ludovicianus*

What to look for: A big-headed, stout-bodied 8-inch songbird with a very thick pale yellow bill. Males are much more colorful than females, being glossy black over the entire head and throat as well as the back, wings, and tail. There are two large white spots (broken wing bars) on the wing. The belly, sides, undertail coverts, and rump are white, and there is a large triangle of bright rose on the upper breast. Females are streaky brown above, white with many brown streaks below, and have five wide white to buffy streaks on the brownish head (one down the center of the crown and two on each side of the head); there are wide white wing bars. Males have rosy red wing linings, but those of females are yellow.

Voice: A loud, fast "cheery-cheery-cheer" something like that of the American Robin, as well as a high-pitched "ink" or "speek" call note. Very vocal.

Behavior: These are birds of woodlands and thickets usually near water. Males sing while on an often hidden perch and also while slowly flying from tree to tree; they also sing while on the nest taking their turn incubating the eggs.

Attracting and feeding: Rose-breasted Grosbeaks are famous feeders on sunflower seeds but also will take peanuts, smaller seeds, mixes, and fruit. They often visit feeders.

Range: This is a familiar breeding bird from central Canada and across the northeastern U.S. south to Kansas and the Appalachians. It spends the winter in Central and South America.

Black-headed Grosbeak • *Pheucticus melanocephalus*

What to look for: Similar in size and shape to the Rose-breasted Grosbeak, the Black-headed once was considered to be a western subspecies of that species. Females are virtually indistinguishable, though they have brighter yellow wing linings and more finely streaked breasts and sides. Breeding males look quite different, however, being basically black on the head, back, wings, and tail, with bright cinnamon underparts and rump plus a broad collar between the head and back. In both sexes red is absent, and males have yellow wing linings like females. The bill tends to be blackish in both sexes. The white to buffy wing bars are prominent in males, smaller in females.

Voice: Generally similar to the song of the American Robin or Rose-breasted Grosbeak, but more whistly and rolling up and down. The call note usually is a loud "spink." Very vocal.

Behavior: Black-headed Grosbeaks are common birds in woodlands, parks, and pasture edges.

Attracting and feeding: These large and distinctive birds often visit feeders, taking a variety of seeds and fruits; they also come to water baths.

Range: An often abundant breeding bird over much of the U.S. west of the Great Plains and central Texas, the Black-headed Grosbeak winters in Mexico but occasionally appears at feeders in the East in autumn and winter.

Blue Grosbeak • *Guiraca caerulea*

What to look for: These very dark 7-inch birds have extremely heavy blackish bills and lack white wing bars. The sexes are very different in color. Males are deep purplish blue above and below, often appearing black when back-lighted, with blackish wings and a small black mask. There is a bright rusty brown anterior wing bar, usually a second less defined buffy wing bar, and many of the other wing feathers are edged with pale tan. Females are brown above and below with darker wings, two rusty brown wing bars (often hard to see), and sometimes a bluish tinge to the rump. Young males are like females but with blue patches, especially on the head.

Voice: Hard to describe, the song is a rich warble that rises and falls. The very loud "chink" call note is fairly distinctive.

Behavior: Blue Grosbeaks tend to inhabit open woodlands, parks, and shrubs near rural roads. They often sit on power lines or on exposed perches. If you watch long enough, you are sure to see the bird flick and spread the tail feathers.

Attracting and feeding: Though seldom common, Blue Grosbeaks occasionally visit feeders, taking a wide variety of seeds.

Range: Blue Grosbeaks are breeding birds across all but the northern tier of states and southern Florida. They winter in the Caribbean and Central America.

Lazuli Bunting • *Passerina amoena*

What to look for: A compact 6-inch bird with a large head and rather small, conical gray bill. Males are bright blue from the head over the back to the base of the tail, with blacker wings and tail. There are two white wing bars, one wide, the other narrow. The throat is blue, the breast and flanks bright orange, and the belly white. Females are brown over the head and back, with a faintly blue rump; the wings and tail are blacker, and there are two pale wing bars. The throat and breast are washed with buffy.

Voice: The song is a fast, musical series of rising and falling notes, often in pairs, and ending with a chatter or jumble of notes.

Behavior: These pretty little birds are most common in open woodlands, shrubby areas, and the edges of pastures and parks, often where water is present. Males often sing from exposed perches.

Attracting and feeding: Like other buntings, Lazuli Buntings often visit feeders to take a variety of small seeds. They also use birdbaths.

Range: Lazuli Buntings breed over the northwestern U.S. from the Great Plains to Washington and south to New Mexico and California. They winter south to Mexico.

Indigo Bunting • *Passerina cyanea*

What to look for: Indigo Buntings are small (5.5 inches long), rather plump and big-headed birds with short but thick, conical bills. Adult males are deep blue above and below, darker on the wings and tail, the wing feathers often edged with buffy. Females are brown above and buffy below with indistinct darker streaks; the wings and tail are darker, and sometimes two buffy wing bars can be distinguished. Young males are like females but with patches of blue feathers, especially on the rump and breast; autumn males may appear polka-dotted brown and blue. The bill is black but may appear glossy blue-gray near the lower base.

Voice: The song is a long, rather dry series of doubled notes that rise and drop and often are interrupted by a "buzz" note.

Behavior: Abundant summer birds in the eastern U.S., Indigo Buntings like open areas at the edges of forests and often are seen in flocks in pastures and perched on power lines along rural roads. They often nest in relatively dry areas and adapt well to human modifications of their habitat. Males sing from exposed perches and may be very conspicuous, while females often are skulkers. In the autumn, large flocks of adults and immatures may be found in areas of dry weeds.

Attracting and feeding: Indigo Buntings visit feeders to take small seeds, peanuts, and fruits of all types.

Range: An abundant breeding bird over the entire eastern U.S. from the Dakotas to central Texas and east to the Atlantic, recently also ranging into the southwestern U.S., it winters mostly in tropical America.

Painted Bunting • *Passerina ciris*

What to look for: This small (5.5 inches), rather stout-bodied and big-headed bird may have the most tropical-looking pattern of any U.S. bird. Though females are green, darker above, more yellowish below, males are spectacular. The head is bright sky-blue, the underparts from throat to undertail coverts are bright red, as are the rump and lower back, the back is bright green (yellower in the center), and the wings and tail are brownish with a blue to green sheen; there is a narrow orange eye ring.

Voice: The song is a loud series of often paired notes delivered in a high whistle and usually including the phrase "pew-eeta." There is a loud "chip" call note.

Behavior: For such gaudy birds, they often are difficult to see, flitting through low shrubs and thickets, often near water. In migration they seem to be fond of pastures with thick seeding grasses. Males sing from exposed perches.

Attracting and feeding: Painted Buntings may visit feeders to take a variety of seeds, and it is not uncommon for small flocks or groups of families to make a feeder and birdbath parts of their territories.

Range: This is a bird of the southern states, most likely to be seen from central Texas to Louisiana and north into Missouri; small populations also breed in coastal Georgia and the Carolinas. Painted Buntings winter mostly in Mexico and Central America, but some birds remain in southern Texas, Louisiana, and southern Florida.

Eastern Meadowlark • *Sturnella magna*

What to look for: A 9- to 10-inch bird, the Eastern Meadowlark has a dumpy body, small head with long, sharply pointed bill, and a short tail. The back, wings, and tail are streaked with brown and black, the outer three or four tail feathers white with few dark markings. The underparts are bright yellow from the throat to the belly, the undertail coverts usually pale yellow to white. There is a distinctive black V on the breast. The throat is yellow, not extending onto the face, which is pale buffy to grayish.

Voice: The song is loud, carries well, and distinctive, a four-syllable whistle that is high-pitched and sometimes interpreted as "see-you, see-yeeer."

Behavior: Eastern Meadowlarks are inhabitants of pastures, fields, and, of course, meadows. They fly often, when their short, wide-spread, white-edged tails, yellow underparts with black V, and chunky bodies make them easy to identify. The food consists of insects and other small invertebrates picked from the ground along with grass seeds.

Attracting and feeding: Eastern Meadowlarks seldom come to feeders, though they will take cracked corn during dry weather when insects are sparse. They often dust bathe.

Range: This meadowlark is a year-round resident in the southern U.S. from southeastern Arizona to Florida and north to the Great Lakes; it occurs as a breeding bird north to the Canadian border. The range extends south into northern South America and the West Indies. Migration usually is for only short distances. The Western Meadowlark, found from the Great Lakes area over the Great Plains to the Pacific Coast, is virtually identical in coloration but has a different song of two parts, the first like the song of the Eastern Meadowlark, followed by a long sequence of bubbling chatter. Hybrids occur where the species overlap.

Yellow-headed Blackbird • *Xanthocephalus xanthocephalus*

What to look for: A large (9 to 10 inches) blackbird with a long, rounded tail, relatively long bill, and distinctive coloration. Males are glossy black on the back, wings, tail, and belly, the entire front part of the body being bright yellow except for some black skin around the eye. There is a broad white wing patch visible both in flight and when perched. Females are slate-brown above and below, weakly streaked, with a yellow breast and throat and yellow around the eye. A white wing patch is absent in females.

Voice: A loud, raucous species producing a great number of clucks, screeches, and scraping noises, often preceded by a couple of whistled notes.

Behavior: Yellow-headed Blackbirds form large to huge breeding colonies in marshy areas, often near lakes and wet meadows.

Attracting and feeding: In nature Yellow-heads feed on insects and seeds, so they are easily attracted to feeders.

Range: Yellow-headed Blackbirds nest from southwestern Canada across the central and western U.S. from California to Michigan. The wintering range is mostly in Mexico.

European Starling • *Sturnus vulgaris*

What to look for: This 8-inch "blackbird" is easily recognizable by silhouette: it has a dumpy body, short tail, and long, pointed bill; the legs are long and set well back on the body. In flight, the short wings and short tail combine to produce a wedge-like appearance. Adults are black above and below, the wings and tail browner. Spring adults are glossy black with limited silvery spangling on the back and wings; their bill is bright yellow (males) to pinkish (females). Later in the year the dark edges of most feathers wear off, producing a browner bird that is heavily covered with silvery spangles above and below; the bill becomes black. Young birds are dusky brown with dark bills.

Voice: Starlings usually produce a variety of squeaky calls but sometimes can break into more musical whistles.

Behavior: First introduced into the U.S. from Europe about 1890, European Starlings rapidly spread from their New York point of entry to in less than a century become resident birds over the entire U.S. and southern Canada. They are aggressive birds that form gigantic flocks of sometimes tens of thousands of birds, and they are tree-hole nesters.

Attracting and feeding: If you put soft foods on the ground, you will attract starlings. They feed largely on insects and fruits in nature and show little interest in the usual hard seeds liked by most birds.

Range: Found everywhere in the U.S. though often common only near cities.

Red-winged Blackbird • *Agelaius phoeniceus*

What to look for: An 8- to 9-inch blackbird with a moderately short tail and sharply pointed bill. Females are slate-black to brown above, heavily streaked on the foreparts and underparts with brown on white or buffy; there often are a distinct pale eye brow stripe and buffy throat. Males are glossy black (spotted with buffy in young males and some winter males) above and below with no paler colors except for a large brilliant red patch or badge over the bend of the wing. The red patch usually is followed by a narrower yellow to buffy stripe.

Voice: In addition to a loud "chack" note, male Red-wings produce a loud, hoarse, carrying "konk-a-ree" song.

Behavior: Males develop nesting territories in lowlands. The red shoulder patches seem to allow them to recognize each other as territorial males. Males may start nesting activities several weeks before females arrive on the nesting sites.

Attracting and feeding: Red-wings can show up at feeders any time of the year, varying their insect diet with seeds, suet, and peanut butter mixes. In the winter they often come in large numbers for cracked corn on the ground or low feeding tables.

Range: Red-winged Blackbirds nest over all the U.S. north over much of Canada into Alaska. Those of the central and southern U.S. are year-round residents, though many migrate into Central America in the winter. Tricolored Blackbirds, virtually restricted to California, are almost identical to Red-wings except for the stripe behind the red wing patch being white and differences in calls and behavior.

Brewer's Blackbird • *Euphagus cyanocephalus*

What to look for: A 9- to 10-inch blackbird with a long tail and a sharply pointed bill. The eye is white to yellow in males, brown in females. Adult males are totally glossy black with purple tints on the head and greenish tints on the body. Females are brown overall, the head, nape, and breast often ashy gray.

Voice: A grating "que-cheek" as well as a loud "chick" are produced.

Behavior: A common bird in virtually all types of open habitats in the western U.S., it has become adapted to cities and may be abundant in parks and outdoor markets.

Attracting and feeding: Comes to feeders to take a variety of foods and may become a nuisance.

Range: Brewer's Blackbird breeds from northwestern Canada over much of the western U.S. and is a year-round resident from Arizona to Oregon. In winter is occurs east to the Gulf Coast in Florida. Recently the breeding range has expanded eastward to the Great Lakes area.

Brown-headed Cowbird • *Molothrus ater*

What to look for: A relatively small (7 to 8 inches), conical-billed blackbird often noted wandering in pairs through lawns and forest edges. Females are dull grayish brown, sometimes a bit paler on the head and underparts. Males are glossy black over the entire body and dark brown on the head, nape, and throat.

Voice: The soft, squeaky call often turns into a liquid-sounding bubbly call. Distinctive once heard.

Behavior: A bird of the Great Plains, Brown-headed Cowbirds are adapted to grasslands and have spread east and west as agriculture has removed forests that stood in their way. Females lay their eggs only in the nests of other birds, where they often hatch before the natural inhabitants and grow faster than the natural chicks, causing the parents to waste their energy feeding the cowbird young. Increased numbers of Brown-headed Cowbirds may be a leading cause in the decrease in numbers of many songbirds.

Attracting and feeding: Brown-headed Cowbirds often appear in small numbers at feeders, taking seeds from the ground. Their presence in breeding season often means they are laying in the nests of more colorful songbirds nearby.

Range: Today Brown-headed Cowbirds nest across Canada and the entire U.S. into tropical America. They are year-round residents through the East, South, and Pacific Coast areas. Along the Mexican border to central Texas occurs the Bronzed Cowbird, which is slightly larger with a longer bill and a bright red eye in males.

Common Grackle • *Quiscalus quiscula*

What to look for: A large (a foot or more), long-tailed, sleek blackbird with a heavy, pointed bill. The tail is broadly rounded and dished above near the end, rather spoon-like in flight. Both sexes have bright yellow eyes, but juveniles have brown eyes. Adults are uniformly glossy black above and below, with purple to green iridescence on the head and back. Juveniles are grayish brown. Males and females are about equal in size.

Voice: In addition to a loud "chack" call, a hoarse two-syllable song is produced.

Behavior: Common Grackles are common and easily recognized birds that may occur in small but noisy breeding colonies in parks and the edges of woodlands, usually near water. They feed on insects, fruits, and seeds and will raid the nests of smaller birds. Males strut in front of females, fluffing out the feathers and standing with the wings down and the bill pointed up. Winter flocks may number in the tens of thousands.

Attracting and feeding: Common Grackles feed on almost anything, so they often appear at feeders to take seeds, peanuts, peanut butter mixes, and suet. They usually feed on the ground.

Range: This is a breeding bird over the entire eastern U.S. north into central Canada. The populations from the Great Lakes south are resident year-round, their numbers supplemented in winter by birds from the north. This grackle seldom is found south of the U.S. The Great-tailed Grackle (southern California to Iowa and Louisiana) is over 15 inches long, has an exceptionally long tail, and has a nearly flat head profile.

American Crow • *Corvus brachyrhynchos*

What to look for: American Crows are large (often 18 inches long), uniformly black birds with short tails and very heavy bills. Compared to grackles, these relatives of the jays are much stouter, with larger heads and stronger legs. In flight the tail is evenly rounded at the tip.

Voice: A loud, nasal "caw" is the typical call, but during breeding season American Crows can produce a variety of similar but unexpected calls.

Behavior: American Crows are aggressive birds that feed on almost any type of food, often flying long distances from a protected roosting area to productive feeding grounds. They are flocking birds that may aggregate by the hundreds or even thousands. Crows often raid the nests of other birds and in turn are chased by smaller birds of many types.

Attracting and feeding: Though American Crows will come to feeders for suet and peanuts, they may disturb and harm other birds.

Range: The American Crow is resident through most of the U.S. except parts of the Southwest and breeds north over much of Canada. Similar but smaller species with different voices occur in the Pacific Northwest, Southeast, and Rio Grande basin. Ravens are larger, tend to have heavier bills and ragged crowns, and usually have vaguely triangular tail tips.

Orchard Oriole • *Icterus spurius*

What to look for: Identified as an oriole by the relatively slender body with long tail and long, sharply pointed bill, plus the presence of wing bars and bright colors, the Orchard Oriole is a bit smaller than other common orioles, seldom more than 7 inches long. Adult males are black over the entire head, throat, and breast, as well as over the back, wings, and tail, while the underparts and rump are deep, dark burnt orange. The front wing bar is short and dark orange, the back one white. Females are yellow with a strong green tinge, yellow over the head and underparts, olive above. Males in their first springs (shown) are like females but have a black bib.

Voice: The song is a loud series of musical whistles that fall at the end and often alternate with loud "clucks."

Behavior: Like other orioles, Orchard Orioles are woodland birds, the males often singing from deep within tall trees, but they also are at home in open shrubs and thickets. The nest is a hanging cup of woven grasses as in other orioles but not as long as in some species.

Attracting and feeding: Orchard Orioles seldom come to seeds or suet, but they will visit fruit feeders, including orange halves, and take sugar water.

Range: This is a common breeding species over the entire eastern U.S. from the Great Plains to the Atlantic and southern Canada to the Gulf of Mexico. It winters in tropical America.

Baltimore Oriole • *Icterus galbula*

What to look for: One of our most colorful eastern U.S. birds, the Baltimore Oriole is 8 to 9 inches long. Males are hooded in deep black from the nape to the breast, and the back, tail, and wings are black. The rump and underparts are bright orange, as are the outer tail feathers and the wide front wing bar. Females are yellow below, the belly paler than the breast, and olive from the top of the head over the back. The outer tail feathers are yellowish. Both wing bars are white. Autumn males resemble darkly colored, very bright females.

Voice: The song is an attractive series of musical notes, often flute-like, and one or more "hew-li" notes.

Behavior: Prefers heavily wooded areas, especially near water, to sing and place its long, pendulous nest. Males sing from deep within a heavily leafed tree and may be very difficult to see until they fly to another perch, when the bright orange shines in any light.

Attracting and feeding: If you want to attract Baltimore Orioles, you have to provide fruit, usually oranges but sometimes also pieces of apple, and of couse sugar-water feeders.

Range: The Baltimore Oriole is a common breeding bird from the southern Canadian border south to about Arkansas and North Carolina. Most winter from Mexico to South America, but a few may stay near feeders in the southern states in mild winters. Bullock's Oriole (Great Plains to the Pacific) males have a broad white wing bar, a black crown, and a black stipe though the eye.

Purple Finch • *Carpodacus purpureus*

What to look for: A 6-inch finch with a large, rounded head and short, conical bill. The tail is slightly notched at the tip. Adult males are brown above and white below, including the undertail coverts, brightly stained with rose-red brightest on the crown, face, rump, and the throat and breast; the flanks are lightly spotted, not strongly streaked, with rosy brown. Females and young are brownish with distinct streaking on the underparts; there is a well-defined pale eye brow stripe and often another pale streak back from the base of the bill below a darker eye patch.

Voice: The song is a long, musical warble, interrupted by a sharp "pit" note.

Behavior: These are northern finches that breed in cool coniferous forests and are seen in much of the U.S. only in winter. They tend to feed in trees rather than on the ground, taking buds and fruit as well as seeds and, in spring, insects.

Attracting and feeding: Purple Finches come to feeders in winter, taking a variety of seeds from both hanging feeders and the ground.

Range: Purple Finches breed across Canada and in the mountains of the Pacific Coast and New England. They winter largely in the southeastern U.S., reaching the Gulf Coast states in irruptive years. Cassin's Finch, found in the mountains of the western U.S., is very similar but has a brighter red crown in males with only a faintly rosy breast.

House Finch • *Carpodacus mexicanus*

What to look for: Similar to the Purple Finch but somewhat more slender, with a smaller head in silhouette. There is no distinct pale eye brow stripe in either sex. Males have red over much of the head, throat, breast, and upper belly as well as brown streaking on the undertail coverts. The red is much darker than the rosy hue of the Purple or Cassin's Finch. Females and immatures are heavily streaked above and below.

Voice: A long, loud musical warble like that of a canary, repeating three main syllables. Flocks stay in contact with a loud "wheet" whistle.

Behavior: Though they are birds of forests and lowlands in the western states, in the East they are backyard bird. Males sing from high perches, treetops in the West, power lines and television antennae in the East. Eastern birds seldom are found far from human habitation. Large flocks of immatures and adults form in the late summer and autumn.

Attracting and feeding: A common feeder bird everywhere, eating a variety of seeds, from millet to thistle.

Range: Originally a year-round resident of the western U.S. south into Mexico, a few birds were released on Long Island, New York, in the 1940's. Western populations appear to be moving eastward, and they have come into contact with the westward-moving introduced populations within the last 20 years to completely cover the U.S. They are less common in the southern states but may appear in large flocks in the winter.

House Sparrow • *Passer domesticus*

What to look for: A chunky, big-headed 6-inch bird with a rather large, conical bill, the House Sparrow actually is an Old World member of the weavers, family Passeridae. Adult males are distinctive, reddish brown above with darker streaks and a golden bar on either side of the back; the wing has a single distinct white wing bar; the rump is grayish. The head has a broad gray stripe through the bright rusty brown crown, the nape is rusty brown, and the face is gray. A black bib with rough edges starts on the chin and may continue onto the upper belly; there may be a narrow white band below the face. Females are duller and lack the strong head pattern and black bib; the face is buffy, with a broad pale stripe through the eye. Females and young usually show at least traces of a broad broken white wing bar, never have streaks on the underparts, and have a strong contrast between brown back and wings and grayish white underparts, all characters distinguishing them from female House Finches.

Voice: The song is a seemingly random grouping of chatter and some short whistles. Noisy when in groups.

Behavior: Introduced into the eastern U.S. around 1850, House Sparrows now are ubiquitous backyard and farmyard birds everywhere in North America. They are always active, feeding and chasing each other, the males courting females with quivering, dragging wings. Males are very aggressive, which leads to constant fights.

Attracting and feeding: House Sparrows will come to any seeds placed in a feeder or on the ground and also will take greens, suet, and peanut butter.

Range: A year-round resident throughout North America, it seldom is found far from human activity.

Common Redpoll • *Carduelis flammea*

What to look for: A small finch (5 inches long), with a dark, strongly forked tail and a whitish body with dark brown to black streaks. In breeding males there is a broad pale pinkish rose band across the breast, a small black spot under the chin, and a rounded rosy red cap at the front of the crown. Females have the cap and traces of the rosy breast, while immatures are browner with little or no red. The undertail coverts are streaked with brown.

Voice: High-pitched trills and chatter, including a dry rattle and a "sweeeet" contact note.

Behavior: Common Redpolls are true northern finches common in the most northern states only during harsh winters when seeds and buds have been sparse in Canadian forests.

Attracting and feeding: If Common Redpolls are present in an area, they are almost certain to be attracted to feeders offering thistle (niger or nyjer) seed and also will take small millet.

Range: Common Redpolls breed around the Arctic Circle and in North America are regular winter birds south only to the U.S.-Canada border. Hoary Redpolls, which are a bit larger and much whiter, with less dark streaking, a white rump, and white undertail coverts, have much the same range and may be found in mixed flocks with Common Redpolls.

Red Crossbill • *Loxia curvirostra*

What to look for: A 6-inch finch with a large head and chunky body; the tail is relatively short and deeply notched. The distinctive bill is large, relatively long, both mandibles ending in narrow projections that cross at the tips. Adult males are brown to blackish on the wings and tail, lack wing bars (or have only faint ones), and are pale rosy red, deeper red, or orange from the crown to the belly and on the back; the undertail coverts are pale and have heavy dark brown spots. Females may be pale yellowish, orange, or dull brown; immatures are streaked with brown.

Voice: As a rule, the song consists of pairs of whistled notes followed by trills. The call note often is a loud "kip-kip-kip."

Behavior: The crossed mandibles developed to make picking pine nuts from their cones easier, but these birds also eat other seeds when they can get them and are not restricted to pine forests.

Attracting and feeding: Red Crossbills often come to feeders, taking peanuts, sunflower seeds, and thistle.

Range: These distinctive birds breed from southern Alaska across Canada, south into New England and throughout the mountains of the western states into Mexico. In winter they may turn up anywhere in the U.S., south even to the Gulf Coast states. The White-winged Crossbill is very similar but has two broad white wing bars plus small white spots on the inner edges of the wing.

Evening Grosbeak • *Coccothraustes vespertinus*

What to look for: A very stout, short-tailed, big-headed finch about 8 inches long. The pale bill is very large and conical. The body is buffy gray (females) to dull brown (males), with bright cinnamon underparts, rump, and forepart of the wing. In the male the head is dark brown with a bright yellow stripe across the forehead and a yellow eye brow stripe that runs from the forehead to behind the eye; females have a narrow dark stripe down from the base of the bill (the malar stripe) that is absent in immatures. The wings and tail are black; there is a single large white rectangle in the secondaries of the male's wing, while in the female there also is a large white bar at the base of the primaries.

Voice: The call note given in flight is a loud "cle-ep." The song is a soft warble.

Behavior: This large northern finch feeds extensively on the seeds of conifers in Arctic and montane regions but wanders widely during the winter. As in most finches, the flight is undulating but fast and jerky. It may form large flocks (often with other northern finches) after breeding.

Attracting and feeding: This big-billed finch feeds on a variety of seeds at feeders but seems to prefer sunflower.

Range: Evening Grosbeaks are permanent residents from northwestern Canada to the Maritime Provinces and northern New England, also living in the mountains of the Pacific Northwest and the Rockies south into Mexico. In winter they may occur almost anywhere in the central U.S. and rarely reach the Gulf Coast.

Pine Siskin • *Carduelis pinus*

What to look for: A small (5 inches), rather slender, heavily black-streaked finch with a deeply notched tail that is dark underneath. The back is buffy brown, the underparts whitish, all heavily covered with narrow, well-spaced black streaks. The wings are dark (brown in females, black in males), with two white wing bars and a bright yellow spot at the base of each primary, which is edged with yellow. In flight there is a wide yellow bar extending across the wing and also a yellow area between the rump and the base of the tail. Juveniles are faintly toned with yellow over the entire body. Pine Siskins look like the streaked young or females of many smaller finches, but notice the narrow bill and bright yellow tinges in the wings and tail.

Voice: The song is a complex and variable string of whistles, trills, and warbles, mixed with a loud "che-ee" note. Often very noisy when flying and feeding.

Behavior: These small finches form nervous flocks that scatter and fly away in jerky, undulating movements when alarmed. Like other northern finches, large flocks may form in the winter.

Attracting and feeding: Pine Siskins often descend on feeders in large numbers in the winter, taking quantities of thistle and other small seeds. Easy to attract if in the area.

Range: Pine Siskins are year-round residents in the mountains of the West and also in New England, but they breed north into Alaska. In winter, a few to many birds may appear almost anywhere.

American Goldfinch • *Carduelis tristis*

What to look for: This 5-inch finch has a small, conical bill and a black tail and white rump in all plumages. Breeding males are striking bright yellow birds with a round black cap over the base of the bill and black wings with two white wing bars (the front one a wide patch tinged with yellow) and white feather edges. From autumn to spring they resemble females in being brown above and pale yellow below; winter females may have nearly white bellies.

Voice: A fast series of a variety of high-pitched trills, chatter, and whistles.

Behavior: Common and familiar birds, American Goldfinches often are first noted as they spin by overhead in a fast, erratic, up and down flight, chattering and whining all the time. The birds often feed on flowers and seed heads of thistles and sunflowers

Attracting and feeding: American Goldfinches are among the most reliable of feeder birds, taking thistle and other seeds all year.

Range: Breeding across southern Canada and the northern two-thirds of the U.S. from coast to coast, American Goldfinches are year-round residents from the Great Lakes to Arkansas and winter migrants south to the Gulf Coast and Mexican border. The Lesser Goldfinch (central Texas to Oregon) has yellowish undertail converts (white in American); males have a black or brown back and a solid black crown.

INDEX

Page numbers in **bold** indicate identification discussions; numbers in *italics* indicate other photos

Accipitridae (hawks), 24-25
Aegithalidae (bushtits), 26
Anatidae (ducks), 24
Behavior and identification, 19
Binoculars, types, 9-12
Blackbird, Brewer's, **59**
Blackbird, Red-winged, **59**
Blackbird, Tricolored, 59
Blackbird, Yellow-headed, *23*, **58**
Bluebird, Eastern, **49**
Bluebird, Mountain, 49
Bluebird, Western, 49
Bobwhite, Northern, *25*, **35**
Bombycillidae (waxwings), 27
Bunting, Indigo, **57**
Bunting, Lazuli, **57**
Bunting, Painted, **57**
Bushtit, **45**
Cardinal, Northern, **55**
Cardinalidae (cardinals), 29
Certhidae (creepers), 26
Chickadee, Black-capped, **43**
Chickadee, Carolina, **44**
Chickadee, Chestnut-backed, **44**
Chickadee, Mountain, **44**
Coloration and identification, 18-19
Columbidae (pigeons), 25
Corvidae (jays), 26
Cowbird, Bronzed, 59
Cowbird, Brown-headed, **59**
Creeper, Brown, **46**
Crossbill, Red, **62**
Crossbill, White-winged, 62
Crow, American, **60**
Dove, Inca, **36**
Dove, Mourning, **36**
Dove, Rock, **36**
Dove, White-winged, 36
Duck, Wood, *32*
Emberizidae (sparrows), 28-29
Families of birds, 23ff
Field guides, 12-13
Finch, Cassin's, 61
Finch, House, **61**
Finch, Purple, **61**
Flicker, Gilded, 39
Flicker, Northern, **39**
Flycatcher, Ash-throated, **40**
Flycatcher, Great Crested, 40
Flycatcher, Vermilion, *3*, **52**
Fringillidae (goldfinches), 29
Gnatcatcher, Blue-gray, **48**
Goldfinch, American, *16*, **63**
Goldfinch, Lesser, 63
Goose, Canada, **34**
Grackle, Common, **60**
Grackle, Great-tailed, 60
Grosbeak, Black-headed, **56**
Grosbeak, Blue, *20*, **56**

Grosbeak, Evening, **63**
Grosbeak, Rose-breasted, **56**
Hawk, Cooper's, 34
Hawk, Sharp-shinned, **34**
Hirundinidae (swallows), 26
Hummingbird, Anna's, **37**
Hummingbird, Black-chinned, 37
Hummingbird, Broad-tailed, *17*, **37**
Hummingbird, Calliope, 37
Hummingbird, Ruby-throated, **37**
Icteridae (blackbirds), 29
Identification clues, 16-17
Identification techniques, 20
Jay, Blue, **41**
Jay, Steller's, 41
Junco, Dark-eyed, **54**
Kestrel, *24*
Kingbird, Eastern, **41**
Kingbird, Western, **41**
Kinglet, Golden-crowned, **47**
Kinglet, Ruby-crowned, *22*, **48**
Life list, 7
Magpie, Black-billed, **42**
Magpie, Yellow-billed, 42
Mallard, *24*, **34**
Martin, Purple, 26, **42**
Meadowlark, Eastern, **58**
Meadowlark, Western, 58
Mimidae (thrashers), 27
Mockingbird, Northern, **49**
Nesting, wrens, 19
Nutcracker, Clark's, *26*
Nuthatch, Brown-headed, 46
Nuthatch, Pygmy, *25*, 46
Nuthatch, Red-breasted, *6*, *18*, **45**
Nuthatch, White-breasted, **46**
Odontophoridae (quails), 25
Oriole, Baltimore, *21*, **61**
Oriole, Bullock's, *19*, 61
Oriole, Orchard, **60**
Paridae (chickadees), 26
Parts of a bird, 16-17
Parulidae (warblers), 28
Passeridae (house sparrows), 29
Phoebe, Black, **40**
Phoebe, Eastern, **40**
Phoebe, Say's, 40
Picidae (woodpeckers), 25
Polioptilidae (gnatcatchers), 27
Pyrrhuloxia, **55**
Quail, California, **35**
Quail, Gambel's, *15*, **35**
Quail, Scaled, **35**
Ravens, 60
Redpoll, Common, **62**
Redpoll, Hoary, 62
Regulidae (kinglets), 27
Robin, American, **48**
Sapsucker, Red-naped, 39

Sapsucker, Yellow-bellied, **39**
Scientific names, 6
Scrub-Jay, Florida, 42
Scrub-Jay, Western, **42**
Siskin, Pine, **63**
Sittidae (nuthatches), 26
Song identification, 13
Sparrow, American Tree, **52**
Sparrow, Chipping, *7*, **52**
Sparrow, Clay-colored, *7*, 52
Sparrow, Field, *28*, 52
Sparrow, Fox, *30*, **53**
Sparrow, Golden-crowned, **54**
Sparrow, House, *29*, **62**
Sparrow, Song, *12*, **53**
Sparrow, White-crowned, **54**
Sparrow, White-throated, *14*, **53**
Spotting scopes, 13
Starling, European, **58**
Sturnidae (starlings), 29
Swallow, Barn, **43**
Swallow, Tree, **43**
Swallow, Violet-green, 43
Tanager, Scarlet, *8*, **51**
Tanager, Summer, **55**
Tanager, Western, 51
Thrasher, Brown, *33*, **50**
Thrasher, Curve-billed, **50**
Thrasher, Long-billed, 50
Thraupidae (tanagers), 28
Titmouse, Bridled, *6*
Titmouse, Juniper, 45
Titmouse, Oak, 45
Titmouse, Tufted, *1*, *31*, **45**
Towhee, Eastern, **49**
Towhee, Spotted, 49
Trochilidae (hummingbirds), 25
Troglodytidae (wrens), 27
Turdidae (thrushes), 27
Tyrannidae (flycatchers), 26
Verdin, 45
Vireo, Red-eyed, *11*
Warbler, Magnolia, 51
Warbler, Yellow, *28*, **51**
Warbler, Yellow-rumped, *5*, **51**
Waxwing, Bohemian, 50
Waxwing, Cedar, *8*, **50**
Wodpecker, Downy, **39**
Woodpecker, Acorn, **38**
Woodpecker, Gila, 38
Woodpecker, Golden-fronted, 38
Woodpecker, Hairy, 39
Woodpecker, Red-bellied, **38**
Woodpecker, Red-headed, **38**
Wren, Bewick's, **47**
Wren, Cactus, *27*, **46**
Wren, Carolina, **47**
Wren, House, **47**
Yard lists, 7